In Her Shoes: Women of Faith

Co-authored by:

Trivia Afraid of Lightning

Ani Hudgens

Becca Tidwell

Tracy Morgan

Cheryl Ginnings

Christan Barnett

Dana Gailey

Elizabeth Mata

India White

Kelsi Mata

Laton Cangelose

Rachel Bailey

Teree Warren

Tina Parmigiano

Vallette Harris

Victoria Soto

Kathy Fogarty

Allison Unger

In Her Shoes: Women of Faith

ISBN-10: 1727664841
ISBN-13: 978-1727664843

TABLE OF CONTENTS

TRIVIA
AFRAID OF
LIGHTNING

Tell us a little about yourself.

Trivia Afraid of Lightning aka Treva was born November 28th, 1977 and grew up in Rapid City, South Dakota to a Native American mother and estranged African American father whom she has never met. Treva was born into and by her First Nations Lakota speaking grandmother and aunt who influenced her perseverance, tenacity and courage to survive the adversity of poverty. All of which helped her withstand ridicule, self-esteem issues and the effects of cultural trauma; at the age of 12 Treva's grandmother passed away suddenly due to aneurysm of the brain. This great adversity in her life would later be used as a motivational tool to liberate others who have suffered the same fate. Treva is a divorced single mother of three children; her eldest a Mariah daughter 21 years of age, and two son's Mayuka age 19 and Reuben who is 7. Treva has overcome the affects and addiction of drugs, alcohol, homelessness, she is a stroke survivor, foster parent, mentor, motivational speaker, and advocate for suicide prevention in her local community; which serves the Native American population on and off the reservation. At the age of 40, Treva current goals will be obtaining her second Master's in Public Health and will also pursue her PhD in Prevention Sciences and will continue to make an impactable change on a larger scale in the Native American community local and nationwide

Share with us what your business/ministry is and what it does for those that you serve.

Growing up in the culture I was born into. I naturally was gifted in prayer, affirmation, motivation, tenacity and a warrior leadership personality. Every adversity, risky behavior, and statistic that a First

Nations-Native American child, adolescent, adult would experience and have to endure has become my business and ministry, all of which has been from painful traumatic experiences from birth to even present. This great adversity has been a blessing in being a motivational speaker, mentor and foster parent in my in my community and surrounding Indian Reservations in South Dakota.

My life experiences all seem to fall within the same category of business and or ministry, I can minister, and I am able to provide financially for my family! During my undergrad years I had the opportunity to work closely with the Native American demographic in the areas of research and evaluation. During those six years of my college career, I realized this was the ground work for intercessory prayer and regular fasting. This quickly became a new habit for me and my new career path choices (ordered footsteps by God). During my graduate years I had the wonderful opportunity to work directly with the community in the areas of trauma, which was in the areas of historical trauma, personal and cultural healing. I was able to go straight to the areas of need using the gift of discernment and intercessory prayer, also using the cultural perspective of First Nations-Native American "finding your identity" which leads to identity in Christ. Anyone I am blessed to meet is ordained by God himself, and there is no mistake in that.

I am a strong believer we as living walking spirits attract each other in every which way, the light of Christ in us attracts those who are searching. The area in which I serve has always been single parents (both female and male), First Nations-Native American people, and displaced children. With God's continual guidance people receive the foundation to identity, healing and research and to come out of poverty mentality, behavioral issues, and addiction. Ministry in the name of Jesus Christ and research and evaluation people are now understanding how to stay free and come out of generational curses. This is what makes waking up and going to bed late often worth putting in a workday and workweek. I would not change life's circumstances or my job for anything else!

DIRECTION - Sometimes people are confused in recognizing and knowing what they are called to do by the Lord. What advice would you share in how one can hear and know what God has called them to do?

I do believe without a shadow of a doubt, gifting and calling are circumstantial. For example, you may find that you are able to reach, teach, motivate or even love in ways others are unable to d Due to trauma or past violations or victories you have encountered throughout your life and or season's, know and trust it is for the victory of the Lord! This is not only circumstantial but unique because God's has given you the specific ability to be able to bare the test, trial burden and heart ache in your gifting. **John 10:10** "The thief cometh not but to steal and to kill and to destroy. I am come that they might have life, and that they might have it more abundantly". Knowing what you have endured gives your life abundantly! This is an awesome promise from God.

First and foremost, ask and seek the Lord in prayer of your destiny, your spiritual calling in life. I can recall an example I had as a young Christian on fire and filled with zeal and ambition to go forth in ministry. I eagerly reached out to do nursery ministry granted I was a mother of two small children, diaper changing, bottle feeding, and the screams of babies ages birth to about 24 months was not my gifting at that moment in time. **Ephesians 2:10** "For we are his workmanship, created in Christ Jesus for good works, which God prepared beforehand that we should walk in them". God know exactly where we're going and what we are to become!

Often searching for your calling, we are quick to put ourselves in places we are not meant to be. Be mindful of wanting to be involved versus your operating in your calling. Distinguish your talents and abilities and go forth in those areas. When we are in prayer and we are discerning to hear from the Lord there is no harm in testing yourself in the area you're gifted in. I've always said to myself "okay Lord, you didn't answer, you didn't say yes, and you didn't say no... I will be patient and wait and watch for you".

Philippians 2:13 "For God is working in you, giving you the desire and the power to do what pleases him." Your calling and gifting will be ever so pleasing to our heavenly father, remember your pain was not in vain.

I was blessed to have awesome spiritual parents the late Bishop Lorenzo Kelly and First lady Evelyn Kelly in my walk-in ministry, I was also mentored in the ways of intercessory prayer by our church's State Supervisor Mother Cleo Willis. It would be wise to surround yourself with individuals that are operating in their own calling. **Proverbs 19:20** "Listen to counsel and receive instruction, that you may be wise in your latter days".

Here is a small quick recap of advice I found worked for myself and current mentees I work with in ministry and in the community.

1. Look over the adversity or circumstances of your life.
2. Seek the Lord in prayer, wait, watch, and DON'T worry but believe your purpose will be pleasing to the Lord.
3. Look over your current talents and abilities.
4. Surround yourself with like-minded wise believer of Christ or leadership.

DIRECTION – There are times when someone may struggle with really knowing their gifts and how to use them. How did you know what you were gifted in, and how do you apply that in your life?

As mentioned beforehand I believe that gifting is circumstantial, usually ends with it being an utmost desire. Be ever so mindful and pay attention to what your driving force, what is drawing you, and what excites you. First and foremost, seek the lord in your gifting as I mentioned before. All I knew is I wanted to help people to be free from hindering issues that I had endured from birth to young adulthood. I did not know that I had the gift of evangelism, and prophecy. It was pointed out to me later that my desire to be close to the Lord, my prayer according to God's purposes and eventually hearing him and praying "thus saith the Lord'. I began to pray spontaneously for people, situations and even declaring victories in traumatic situations for individuals saying, "In the name of Jesus". Also, discovering that I was operating in wisdom and knowledge that it was nothing from my own insight but the Lord. I doubted of course because the enemy always tries to weaken what God strengthens, but before the doubt would spread like a cancer, we must turn over the doubt and struggle to God, surrender it fully! The enemy of the mind will often cause us to question our gifts. You must be aware when you're questioning it but your zeal and excitement in doing it conflict against each other, then recognize those are two opposites and are chaotic and confusing. **1 Corinthians 14:33** For God is not *the author* of confusion, but of peace, as in all churches of the saints.

Simply ask the Lord to reveal those prophetic words given by him back to you! I asked the lord this in a simple quick prayer. Now, I struggled with this because what the Lord uttered to me was crazy to me at that time and so unbelievable! My faith was tested, and I trusted God and did what I was gifted to do. Someone that I prayed for and prophesied to in the name of Jesus would come to testify what the Lord had done for them tears in their eyes of joy as they rejoiced was solid confirmation of what my gifting was. I rejoiced for her AND rejoiced because I wasn't crazy and willy nilly speaking out of the air! I truly began to fully operate in my gifting in situations I least expected, I had to learn that you cannot put stipulations on the handy work of the Lord. God ordained every situation by his hand, for his glory to be revealed and what I mean by that is I had spiritual guidance from leadership and my spiritual father Bishop Kelly in using wisdom and how to properly operate in my gifting. Depending on your gifting it can be applied in everyday life situations, such as in leadership whether it be in or out the workplace, with your children, husbands, family and community. Never put God in a box in how and where you will use your gifting and with wisdom when using it. When I made the statement "in and out of the workplace" I must clarify that I did not run around the office speaking in tongues, laying hands on people or dowsing clients and employees with holy oil. God operates in order and not in chaos, and in complete peace and wisdom. Use wisdom in knowing when and where the proper times to utter the words of the Lord. In the workplace often, the Holy Spirit will give me the spirit of discernment and with wisdom how to go before specific situations. Gifting comes with patience, listening, trusting and the willingness to act upon his command.

DIRECTION - Many people struggle with developing a habit of including God in all that they do. How do you make God a part of your life/business/ministry each day?

I am a strong believer of self-care, meaning to concentrate on yourself and care for yourself in the areas of mind, body and soul. Prayer can be done even when we think we are not praying. I incorporate prayer and meditation time while working out. There are times when the church body calls for corporate fasting and prayer and have specific times for that. But for personal self-care God wants us to be wholly free and to live this life abundantly. Rule of thumb is to not stress in wondering or thinking "am I praying enough, am I reading my word enough? Let the Holy Spirit continue to draw you near. if you are concerned in this matter. I would suggest concentrating on a scripture weekly and find a way to apply it to your life. Remember this, when you wake up and utter "thank you Lord for waking me up", that is a connection you have! I usually wake up between 5 and 5:30 am and for at least 30 minutes to an hour I concentrate on prayer and silence with the Lord. I physically drink water and seek out early in the morning my spiritual water of life which is my heavenly father. If you're first starting out in developing a habit with staying connected, I would suggest early in the morning or late at night. Choose one that you can connect with more, then make it a habit. Set your clock, cellphone, or anything to notify you to prepare yourself to have that one on with the Lord. Do this until it becomes habit forming. It took me about a week and now it's just a part of my regular waking schedule. I have found that in all I do I follow the standard of being honest, moral, ethical and if I am unable to be any of those on a regular day or every day in private and in public then I should do some self-reflection. We are all human and each have different personality traits but being called by God requires us to put away the old way of thinking, old way of reacting. Emulation of Christ like characteristics are how I incorporate God in all I do in everyday life, with day to day business and with ministry. Again, DO NOT STRESS and feel you are not including God in everything you do. If you are following your destiny and you are being drawn and seeking him in all you do. I believe you're including God in your day to day activities.

FAITH - As a woman of faith, what has been your biggest obstacle or challenge in your faith walk with God, and how did you navigate that successfully?

My biggest obstacle was learning to be ALONE. I am a divorced single parent and there were times I had gone through situations and I needed comfort. I was specific in the type of comfort, I wanted - male companionship. I was surrounded by prayer partners and sisters in the Lord. Do you think that would suffice me? Oh no! I would complain in my struggle and say, "I wished I had a husband to comfort me!" or "I am so alone in this!" Yes, yes whining, kicking and the disrespect in my spirit to utter the word "wish" and not content in what God was trying to accomplish in my life at that time. I had to learn TRUST and know that I was not alone. I had to self-reflect and re-visit some trauma the Lord healed me from that reared itself during a test. I needed to learn to trust God with my mind, my heart, and with my flesh. It was easy to give my mind and heart in prayer, but not the flesh. The flesh is one to be reckoned with, and it will lie to you! I do not trust my flesh as far as I can throw it, and I am a big girl... **Romans 8:12-13** Therefore, brethren, we are debtors, not to the flesh, to live after the flesh. For if ye live after the flesh, ye shall die: but if ye through the Spirit do mortify the deeds of the body, ye shall live.

There was a specific reason I struggled and was physically alone in every trial and adversity I faced. I allowed God to use everything to his glory and can testify that your best outcomes in life happen when you're alone with God and learning to trust him. I am going to be honest and say I do not feel it was navigated the way I would have liked. At the time I felt like I had to fail, fail, fail, and fail again until I was able to learn to trust God without complaint, without doubt, without stress and without control of my flesh then it became successful. Now I can say when I feel alone, I quote scripture and tell the Lord I am thankful in my single situation. I thank you Lord for allowing me the time to be alone in this season. The enemy will always circle back your biggest obstacle in your faith walk. If I allowed my tantrums and whining I would never have been better but bitter, and not able to properly minister to single parent women who struggle with addictions, homelessness, and with suicidal ideations. I have learned to look at the vision and try to envision what God is trying to do and yet he ceases to amaze me with going over and beyond.

FAITH – Many people struggle with having faith when things around them seem to go awry. What would you advise someone who wants to strengthen their faith?

I have learned when struggling with faith when things literally are falling apart. I immediately become positive in my mental patterns! **Proverbs 23:7** for as he thinketh in his heart, so is he: Eat and drink, saith he to thee; but his heart is not with thee. Declare to yourself positive encouraging affirmations Such as, you're a woman or man of great faith. Think and say positive affirmations to yourself, I believe when we get into the habit to think, speak and declare the word of God during a struggle it strengthens our minds to become more resilient against negative self-talk during the struggle. It is our natural reaction to become negative with the negative situations that engulfs us. Secondly, I access my surrounding situations. Did I put myself in this tested struggle or is this enemy driven? Be mindful of your surroundings. Are you constantly watching reality tv that is drama driven? Who you are not ministering to? Are they close coworkers, friends or family? Thirdly, I ask the Lord to strengthen my faith and the will of the Lord. Fourth, I bind the enemy from devouring me in my time of need. I usually end with praising God for strengthening my faith and correcting the situation. I may not see it, but I will do it anyway out of FAITH and believing my faith is being increased and every situation is victorious. Always think, pray and say positive affirmations to yourself and speak into the atmosphere. I cannot reiterate that enough, you will begin to see your faith build, your spiritual strength increase, and doubt dissipate completely.

OVERCOME - How do you structure your time to reflect all the priorities and opportunities God has given you to be a light for him without losing yourself in the process, both personally and professionally?

When opportunities present themselves, I ask the Lord to specifically ordain them for me so that I can do his work in an excellent way according to how he would want it done and without fail. In everything I do, I do in prayer. I do this because I am a single parent, foster parent, active community volunteer and do not want to lose who I am or miss the opportunity to minister to someone. Just because an opportunity presents itself in a perfect way, doesn't not necessarily mean to jump on it. Priorities take precedence, I always check to see if it will affect my children regular day or school week if during the school year. I also need to be mindful it does not conflict with a regular working schedule. Structuring prayer, using discernment and wisdom really are great keys to making decisions when opportunities present themselves.

OVERCOME - Share with us about a season in your life that God sent you through that changed the course of your life.

There have been so many seasons that have changed my life and it is difficult to narrow one down that was life changing. The season of my life I choose to focus on would be the season I experienced the death of a marriage. I was broken, bitter, angry, and couldn't see past the pain. During this season I was completely in a backslidden state, an overeater, alcoholic, became a drug addict and was 100% violent. I was full of rage and in a constant state of self-destruction with no recourse of healing which lead to depression and suicidal ideations. I was going through such loss and disbelief in a marriage I had hope and prayed for. I was literally at the end of the road. I was at my heaviest of 400 plus pounds and a regular cocaine user; a recipe for a complete cardiac arrest. By the grace of God, he literally kept me from the hand of the enemy and gave me a chance to live out my destiny. I remember the day I asked the Lord to heal my heart. I asked, cried and pleaded "help me please to be better, I am tired of being bitter". The willingness to surrender to the Lord not only set me free but placed me on a ministering path and a career path in higher education that was all part of his glorious master plan. I imagine what would have happened if I had not cried that prayer. My children would have been motherless. I would have been strung out on numerous drugs, homeless, not in my right mind and without a shadow of a doubt - dead! I literally bless, praise and have tears of joy knowing that God's plan for my life is greater than what the enemy had planned His plan was more than what I could even imagine. I came out of that season restored, onto a path of mentoring single parents, and being better and not bitter!

POUR -What three scriptures would you share with someone if they are in a season of transition and need clarity? Also, share why you selected these three scriptures. I

I have learned that I had to become my own cheerleader and motivator. I researched scriptures that gave me hope, promise and strength in knowing that I am victorious in God's promises.

Philippians 3:14 speaks of pressing toward. While you're transitioning during a season there is always an end goal. I always visualized pushing forward in every way, such as emotion, prayer, at work, and with family matters. Sometimes transitioning is easy and wonderful in some seasons. The seasons of maturity and growth are the seasons that may be uncomfortable and painful. Those seasons are the seasons I am referring to.

Philippians 3:14 I press toward the mark for the prize of the high calling of God in Christ Jesus.

Psalms 119:30-32 also encouraged me to have a made-up mind always and especially during your transition, there is always a blessing and with that blessing there is responsibility. Chose to stay under the umbrella of Lord, following his commandments.

Psalm 119:30-33 I have chosen the way of truth: thy judgments have I laid before me. I have stuck unto thy testimonies: O Lord, put me not to shame. I will run the way of thy commandments, when thou shalt enlarge my heart. Teach me, O Lord, the way of thy statutes; and I shall keep it unto the end.

Finally, **Colossians 3:2** was a constant reminder to seek heaven and to think heaven bound! I realized early into my walk with the Lord that your thought pattern during any kind of transition whether it be positive or negative should always be positive.

Colossians 3:2 Set your affection on things above, not on things on the earth.

POUR -What is your favorite scripture, and how has that influenced your role as a woman who works and walks by faith?

I love the word of God, always so positive and promising it is a never-failing living word! **Isiah 41:10** Fear thou not; for I am with thee: be not dismayed; for I am thy God: I will strengthen thee; yea, I will help thee; yea, I will uphold thee with the right hand of my righteousness. One of my favorites! This verse is a firm reminder God is God and in control, and he is my strength and holds me with his righteous right hand! This lets me know walking by faith I am always victorious! A promise! This leaves me confident, at peace and rested in knowing who my Father is and the influence he gives through his word.

ANI
HUDGENS

Tell us a little about yourself.

My name is Ana Veronica Hudgens, friends and family call me "Ani." I was born in Havana, Cuba. My parents brought me to the United States of America in February 1969, when I was only seventeen months old. I don't remember anything about Cuba, however, my parents made sure I was raised with some very strong "old school" values. My Cuban heritage and traditions run deep. My mother was adamant that I master English and Spanish-she made sure I learned to speak, read, and write both properly. She taught me to be self-sufficient, courageous, and independent. My father was the strict disciplinarian, always reminding me of *my name* and where I came from. Growing up, I resented his strict rules and discipline, so I rebelled-yet he taught me the meaning and importance of a zealous work ethic, and how to be a leader rather than a follower. I was raised Catholic, and from a young age, I struggled for answers to questions that didn't align with the sense of blind faith felt with every heartbeat.

Life for as long as I can remember has felt like a never-ending rollercoaster of chaos: I'm a wife, mom, daughter, sister, aunt, Godmother, friend, volunteer and advocate in my community, founder of a non-profit educational program, and entrepreneur. Overall, life has been *complicated*: endless obstacles and an overwhelming sense of exhaustion. Since I was a ten-year-old latchkey kid, I've worn many hats, sometimes even a tiara or crown (*really, I have*, lol, but that's another story) a lifetime of responsibilities, stress, and self-inflicted heartache because somewhere in my DNA there is a glitch that compels me to think I am responsible for fixing everything and everyone around me.

A long time ago, I stepped into the role of being the foundation of strength and responsibility for my family and friends. I'm the one who gets things done; who is quick to volunteer when someone needs help; who works endless hours for causes and charities; who helps the less fortunate, the hurt, the sad, the lost, the ill, etc. My bff/soul sister, Margarita Santiago, once told me she sees me as the Patron Saint of *everyone*, and I didn't quite understand what she meant. Was it a compliment or a wakeup call? Quite honestly, I still haven't figured it out, but it did help me step back and have a very raw and honest conversation with myself leading to the 5th of September 2017. I was not just *blessed* with another day of life. That day had extra significance because it was my fiftieth birthday. Ironically, when I woke up that morning, I didn't remember it was my birthday until I reached for my beautiful pink bible on my nightstand-a very important part of my morning routine (*best gift ever* thanks to my sweet friend Daisy Vega's giving heart). When I opened my bible that morning, a small pink envelope fell out. I recognized it yet couldn't remember when I put it there. It was a birthday card to *me* from *me*:

"Dear Ani, today is your 50th birthday! This is it kiddo...you have been BLESSED with 18,250 days of life. You've been successful in business. You're an awesome wife, mother, daughter, sister, and friend, but this is it-time to be honest *with yourself and start living the life God has planned for you. You've become pretty good at faking it to the world around you as if everything is good, and you wear a huge smile every day to keep others from seeing how deep you have pushed the pain and sorrow you have survived into your soul. You are fearfully and wonderfully made. You are unique, whole, precious, strong, beautiful, worthy, and redeemed! Today, you will break the chains and start celebrating the truth; every struggle and every blessing in your life-it's* all *part of who you are.*

It's time to start working on the masterpiece which is you. Yes, you're also a work in progress, but this is a reminder you can be both at the same time. God has an amazing plan for your life and the time has come. It's time for you-physically, mentally, emotionally, and spiritually-to remove yourself from the backburner and walk in faith 200%, even when you cannot see! Happy 50th Birthday, BeYOUtiful…it's time to take who you are, who you want to be, and what you can do and use it for a purpose that is greater than you. It is time to set yourself free and live the life you were born for! With Love…xoxoxox!!!"

Share with us what your business/ministry is and what it does for those that you serve.

For twenty-five years, my personal and professional goals were ambitious. Yet, as a corporate Human Resources Director, I was working endless hours to meet or exceed the requirements of my position. Back then, my "career" was everything; it provided for my family-however, I was sacrificing so much: my family, my health, my dreams, and my integrity. Regardless of my intentions and loyalty to the companies and employees I worked for, it was never enough. Yet, I refused to give up or make the changes I knew my heart and soul yearned for. But all my long-term goals and plans were obliterated in May 2010 when I was almost killed in an auto accident. In the blink of an eye, my body, my mind, and my spirit where crushed. I felt so lost. How was I going to provide for my family? For the first three years following the accident, I fought to hold on to my faith. I had very dark days full of pain, long conversations, and many one-sided arguments with God demanding answers-not to why this had happened to me, just a lot of: "Now what? Here I am, completely surrendering-please take this and show me what You want me to do. I will do it. You spared me, so there must be a reason. Whatever Your plan is, that must be it. It's time for me to get out into the world, share my story, educate families, and do my part to save lives, one child at a time. Seatbelt safety was definitely a cause, and I will not be afraid, so **lead me**!" As I mourned the death of who I used to be, I sought out a purpose. If I was still alive, it was for a reason. Seat Belt Safety? If I had not been buckled up, I would not be alive, so yes, I was very passionate about it, but little did I realize that during the four years I poured all my energy into The Miss Buckle-Up Princess Foundation, God had an additional plan for my life. I needed to conquer the ongoing challenges leading to my deteriorating health. I was sick and tired of being sick and tired when I was led to the incomparable Sheryl Duchess, N.D., M.H. blessing my life as a mentor, taking me under her wing, and inspiring me to become a Certified Naturopathic Wellness Coach. I am committed to empowering others on their journey to optimal health through education, prevention, and awareness. I help incorporate natural methods to enhance good health and encourage longevity with an emphasis on disease prevention. Every day, I do my best to serve my clients through hope, kindness, compassion, devotion, and love.

Sometimes, people are confused in recognizing and knowing what they are called to do by the Lord. What advice would you share in how one can hear and know what God has called them to do?

God is constantly speaking to us! For many years, I missed out on hearing God's message because I was not devoted to making my relationship with God a priority in every part of my life. I lost my way, wasting too many years walking in the flesh and only seeking God's guidance during a crisis or when facing major decisions. When our lives turn into an endless war of frustration, when we are consumed by stress and confusion, when we are in dire need of hearing the Lord's message and recognizing what He is calling us to do, there is no way we can recognize-much less hear-what we should do. We must learn to develop our relationship with God-an empowering and transforming relationship where we are spiritually mature and close to Him every day!

There are times when someone may struggle with really knowing her gifts and how to use them. How did you know what you were gifted in, and how do you apply that in your life?

Looking back on my life, I can now identify the gifts God blessed me with at a very young age. However, that wasn't always the case. I clearly remember being in Catholic school and getting in trouble during catechism class because at the age of seven, I was an outspoken, precocious little girl with a serving heart. Many times, I was told I was to speak only when spoken to, that no one liked a "smarty pants," much less a bossy young lady. Even at home, I was told I had to tone it down, mind my words, and do as I was told. Years later, I embraced my God-given gifts-applying them to my career, my service to others in my community, and in empowering girls and women of all ages to recognize they are each "fearfully and wonderfully made!" God blesses each of us with different talents, abilities, independent qualities, and gifts: wisdom, knowledge, faith, healing, and prophecy-many seemingly natural abilities, and other more miraculous ones. I praise God for my **voice**-even when I could not speak!

Many people struggle with developing a habit of including God in all that they do. How do you make God a part of your life/business/ministry each day?

Every morning when I open my eyes, I thank God for the blessing of another day. Each day, I praise him for **everything** in my life-the good, the not-so-good, and even the ugly. I cannot and will not get out of bed without a daily devotion. What may seem insane to some is a way of life for me. I'm practically on speed dial with God for everything in my life. I'm in constant conversation/prayer with Him. I pray before and after all networking events, meetings, seminars, and speaking engagements. I pray as I buckle my seatbelt every time I get in an automobile. I praise God for everyone I cross paths with every day, and I pray for clarity and guidance. I always pray, "Whom may I **bless** today, Lord?" be it a kind word, smile, or hug, helping or inspiring them on their health, wellness, and spiritual journey.

As a woman of faith, what has been your biggest obstacle or challenge in your faith walk with God, and how did you navigate that successfully?

In this life, I have faced many obstacles and challenges. I have been in a tough fight with my health for over forty years. I have battled bulimia, morbid obesity, diabetes, and heart disease. One would think surviving and overcoming debilitating injuries in an auto accident was my biggest obstacle. No! That was a tough journey, but not the biggest challenge in my faith walk with God. In November 2016, my heart was crushed when my husband-who was my rock of love, strength, and support from the day we met-collapsed and was rushed to the hospital. I remember sitting in a very quiet private waiting room for over two hours before a nurse and hospital chaplain came to speak with me. At approximately 1:30 am, I faced the reality that my husband had *not* collapsed due to diabetes (which was my initial thought as panic set in when he stopped breathing while lying on our bedroom floor). The man I loved was in a trauma unit hooked up to endless machines. The man I thought I knew so well was unconscious, was not breathing on his own, had aspirated when he violently vomited. I found myself on my knees sobbing, completely alone trying to make sense of the fact that my husband had a blood alcohol level well over .50 and might not ever wake up again. Grim reality, fear, anger, frustration, and guilt were my companions that long, dark evening after I signed a DNR (Do Not Resuscitate form). I sat at his bedside praying and begging God to spare his life, bring him back to me, allow him to wake up so I can tell him how much I love him, and that-whatever it would take-I would be there for him. God answered my prayers, but soon after, the blinders I had been wearing for so long were gone, and I learned what it meant to love someone who was a binge-drinking, functioning alcoholic since the age of thirteen. My type A personality could not fix this-no matter how much I begged, pleaded, and prayed to God. My husband's depression, self-loathing, suicidal thoughts, and drinking is a disease that only he can get help for. I had to learn to **be still** and listen to the Lord.

Many people struggle with having faith when things around them seem to go awry. What would you advise someone who wants to strengthen their faith?

Grief, pain, depression, anxiety, stress, anger, frustration are all challenges I've faced throughout life where I have caught myself struggling with my faith. My journey has been long, learning to walk by faith even when I cannot see. I would advise to focus on your faith **every day**, not just when times are tough. Focusing on your faith every day is essential to keeping it resilient and getting you through the toughest of times. Do the things that make you strong and bring you peace-working out, reading, music-it's important to nourish your soul and feed your faith. Allow yourself to grieve your losses and acknowledge life's realities. Our cries are heard by an all-listening, Almighty God. When feelings of uncertainty overwhelm you, be patient. We each have a purpose that is created just for us. Be true to yourself; don't rebound or fill in the gaps when life throws you a curve ball. Make certain you are always aligned with your core beliefs and values and surrender to faith-do not resist. Faith doesn't happen by chance or accident. Take action and live a positive life.

How do you structure your time to reflect all the priorities and opportunities God has given you to be a light for Him without losing yourself in the process both personally and professionally?

Start and end every day with prayer! Set aside quiet time and just have a conversation with the Lord. I have lost myself a few times in life's insanity with work, overcommitting to social events, fundraisers, networking, family emergencies, etc. When I allow personal or professional pressures and schedules to interfere, I'm completely unbalanced and unable to share my God's gracious gifts with others.

Share about a season that God sent you through that changed the course of your life.

We all make choices in our lives. Sometimes those choices result in heartache, betrayal, or infidelity, along with physical, emotional, and psychological harm. For many years, I was embarrassed and afraid to be honest about the detrimental choices I've made in life, especially pertaining to relationships and marriage. It's taken a long time for me to openly share my story with others and not be mortified about what they will think or say. I have been married five times. Five different husbands. I have been divorced four times; each relationship was different, corresponding to different stages in my life. As I share this story with you, my heart aches because I recently had to surrender my existing marriage, along with my husband's addiction, into God's capable hands. We are now separated. Every day, I pray my husband finds his way to God. I pray he finds peace and redemption. I am at a crossroads in life; some would say I'm "in limbo," because I do not know what will come. I do know I love my husband with all my heart-and because I love him, I had to walk away. At times, my journey reminds me of the Samaritan woman at the well. Others have been quick to judge me; I have been shunned, criticized, and humiliated by strangers as well as those I thought were my friends, and even family members. Through every season of my life, Jesus has been with me. He knows my history and accepts me with love and compassion.

What three scriptures would you share with someone who is in a season of transition and needs clarity? Also, share why you selected these three scriptures.

Seasons of transition in our lives may include career/job, getting married, starting a new business, going on a mission trip, God's call, school/college, pregnancy, terminal illness, retirement, divorce, or anything that brings change from life's normal routine. Transition, whether negative or positive, sometimes brings feelings of anxiety, fear, worry, uncertainty, indecision, and stress amongst other feelings.

Transition always brings new roles and responsibilities. Sometimes, we must wipe the slate clean and start from scratch, start a new life, form a new routine, establish new relationships, and adjust to a new way of life. The thought of starting over again can be overwhelming and terrifying and is probably why many people are hesitant and procrastinate when it comes to change.

In my lifetime, I have experienced many seasons of transition-some very painful, though all a blessing-even though at the time, I was terrified. Other seasons have been filled with joy, an abundance of love, friends, family, and success. The following scriptures have always helped me find clarity through life's seasons of transition.

Philippians 4:6-7 *Do not be anxious about anything, but in every situation, by prayer and petition, with thanksgiving, present your requests to God. And the peace of God, which transcends all understanding, will guard your hearts and your minds in Christ Jesus.*

Proverbs 3:5 *Trust in the LORD with all your heart, and do not lean on your own understanding.*

Deuteronomy 31:8 *The LORD himself goes before you and will be with you; he will never leave you nor forsake you. Do not be afraid; do not be discouraged.*

What is your favorite scripture, and how has that influenced your role as a woman who works and walks by faith?

The Proverbs 31 Virtuous Woman shines as a bright guiding light in my life. Today, as we see women of all ages following questionable role models, my passion and purpose is to continue living a virtuous life by being an example of responsibility and gumption. I strive to be a woman who embodies the qualities that every believing woman should strive for in her personal and family life, and in her daily work. Proverbs 31: 25-26 sums it up for me: *She is clothed with strength and dignity, and she laughs without fear of the future. When she speaks, her words are wise, and she gives instructions with kindness.*

Closing thoughts?

We are all unique and amazing in our own way. Perfection is a figment of our imagination. Be kind to yourself and the people in your life, be considerate and caring. When you give, give straight from your heart. In doing so, you are gifting yourself and everyone around you. Never forget what a treasure you are in this world. Continue your walk in the faith, inspire, and share your story with others. Our challenges, heartaches, and perseverance are a living example-and someone else's hope.

BECCA TIDWELL

Tell us a little about yourself.

My name is Becca and I am 24 years old, living in New Orleans with my husband Todd, who is my best friend and biggest supporter. We've been clumsily chasing God together for the last few years, 9 months of that married! I grew up in Indiana with my parents and three siblings. I lived in a small town, where kids drove those tractors to school, and I had the same best friend for 24 years, it was that kind of place. I went to the best university with such a wonderful community. I often wonder how to regain that kind of depth in those friendships again. I credit this to the relationships made while I was involved in called Younglife. It is an awesome ministry. If you have not heard of it, Google a Younglife camp video and you'll see why. I am a Fine Arts Major from Purdue University and I love to spend time painting, drawing, crafting, especially for other people, or for the walls of my new home with Todd. I like anything creative, good movies, iced coffee, reading, music, pizza, bubble baths, happy crying, and a good game night with friends that lasts until the wee hours of the morning. Nothing and no one brings me more joy than my little tribe of nieces and nephews!

Share with us what your business/ministry is and what it does for those that you serve.

Although my entire life should scream Jesus without a structured ministry, it helps to have one! I am still involved with Younglife, a Christian ministry that reaches high school kids where they're at with adventure and the Gospel. My ministry began at Purdue University where I sought out girls from a local high school and became their friend. (Which may sound creepy, but they quickly got over that once we started talking.) There are so many kids just looking for someone to show up and be consistent with them. They look for people who want to be their friend, to pick them up for coffee or the football game. These girls were a part of my heart like I had never experienced before, like they were my babies- I always called them that.

My ministry provided me with friends, life-long companions, my bridesmaids in my wedding, and even my husband who I met through Younglife. What better way to bring people together than the captivation of the Gospel? My ministry changed and moved when I did to New Orleans, Louisiana. My girls here are different than Indiana, but they still have my heart in huge ways. So eager, curious, and wanting of a savior. Younglife creates this safe place for my girls. They meet for bible study where they can feel heard. They have a place to offer to God what they have, especially what they're feeling, because emotions are hard! We laugh, we cry, we wonder where God is, we see Him, we read His word, and we lift each other up. I love them so much and I love running towards light with them. When they call late at night because they just got their heart broken, I don't even mind the 5 hours of sleep I'll be missing to sit with them (well, maybe just a little).

My side-hustle is making art, like prints, portraits, wall hangings, jewelry, and selling them from my blog (ordinarilydevout.com), Etsy (etsylazybeez), and Instagram (@ordinarily_devoutart. I value this greatly because I love making orders and seeing people hang, wear, and love their treasures. I've learned a tad about marketing; like the more you post and promote, the more you sell! Makes sense, huh? Anyways, no more plugging my small business, just know that if there is something cool that you create that makes you different than others, MAKE it! Sell it, see where it takes you. On the other side of that, when you need a gift for someone, consider supporting a woman in business by purchasing something from her instead of going to Target. It will make her happy dance all the way to Hobby Lobby.

DIRECTION - Sometimes people are confused in recognizing and knowing what they are called to do by the Lord. What advice would you share in how one can hear and know what God has called them to do?

This is absolutely the realest and most pressing topic in my life right now. My goodness, I don't know if there is a theme that rings truer for me in this very moment. What has the Lord called me to do? This 24-year-old girl desperately wished she knew what her God and Father wanted for her in the long run. This may not be the answer someone is looking for or wants to hear. But while I was writing this, I had to pause because I really had no idea what to do with my life or where God will take me. There was supposed to be this career after college that was perfect, where I made the right amount of money, that I would love and that would help change the world. But that just isn't so. I want to paint, write, dance, dream, act, sing, create, speak life, have lots of babies, own a coffee shop, and teach art therapy. That's what I think I'm good at, and those are things I want. But is that what God wants for me? It seems only natural that the gifts I have are what I would use for His glory and kingdom. Confusion sets in and I wonder will I even be qualified at all to do one thing for the rest of my life? A very wise husband of mine says no, I don't have to be qualified for God to use me. Sigh of relief, even if just for a moment. I've had a few career minded doors close on me lately that left me very disappointed. So, I am in the waiting season waiting to see which door God will open next. Pay attention to your heart's intentions and be open to God saying no to something, even if it hurts to hear. What I am sure of right now is that I am called to love people! No matter when God chooses to reveal our purpose to us, we can love people where we are at now. Don't worry, our life won't be wasted. Your walk, my walk, no matter how crooked or tired our steps, will not be wasted.

DIRECTION – There are times when someone may struggle with really knowing their gifts and how to use them. How did you know what you were gifted in, and how do you apply that in your life?

I found my gifts by staying in touch with my passions and things that make me feel useful and alive. Art has always been something I turn to to express myself, to cheer others up, and to admire beauty and nature. I've always felt as though this was God-given. Reason being, I hear Him when I'm painting. I see Him project creativity onto a page and can feel the most calming presence when I create with my hands.

I try to make things often and when I do, I'm reminded that God, the creator, has allowed me to create- a favorite branch of mine to the never-ending tree that is God. I have been singing since I can remember; in church choirs, school plays, and jam sessions. I really think prayer is one of my gifts; prayers for myself and prayers for other people. Vulnerability is one of my gifts too because I am usually not afraid to be messy and real with friends. I will also cry with you, no matter what about, I will shed actual tears with you if that's what you need! I'd like to think this is a gift, too.

When trying to find your gifts, I would venture to the place in you where God gets the glory. What can you use for him? Sometimes I think we must ask other people what our gifts are. Maybe we don't know or maybe we like to hear it from them to comfort us or confirm it for us. Well, I had to ask. It's okay to ask. Gifts from God can be seen at their brightest and most evident when in community with others; a body where everyone's gifts are complementing another's. If you don't know your gifts or are unsure how to fit them in, join a community!

DIRECTION - Many people struggle with developing a habit of including God in all that they do. How do you make God a part of your life/business/ministry each day?

First, have accountability. For me this takes a few forms. Whether it is a group of younger girls you are walking with who ask you tough questions that keep you studying the Word, or wiser mentors pouring into you by drawing you deeper, seek accountability. If these lovely women are in your life daily, even better!

I ask God to keep my convictions before me, so I am called out quickly when He isn't in my every day. Even if you must force yourself to spend time with Him, do it. Some days I must force myself to click on the worship playlist instead of chill folk rock or oldies. Just click it; you know you will be glad you did. I don't know about you, but with my ministry friends and with Younglife, I can tell when I have faked it through a conversation, convincing myself I have had enough Jesus that day. You realize you need to make it a habit to include Jesus when you're so far away from Him and feeling the spiritual pounds pack on so heavily. It's hard to breathe, you feel sick, and you can't run fast alongside Him the way you want to. Just like a diet or exercise plan, we know when we need one. Usually, when our stomachs hurt, we are out of breath or when we are tired and can't fit into our jeans. Just as you work out your body, work out that spirit! The good thing is, He will walk with us at a slow pace, not ahead of us, while we get into shape with him. This may be devoting one thing to Him every day that takes up time. I pick showers! I must take showers (or at least I should) so why not assign that time to be Jesus time? While in the shower I pray, sing, and reflect on small and big things alike. I'm reminded of how helpless and hopeless we are without a daily interaction with God.

FAITH - As a woman of faith, what has been your biggest obstacle or challenge in your faith walk with God, and how did you navigate that successfully?

Sometimes I feel super old for example, when a show I used to watch when I was little turns 20 years old. Or when kids in high school don't know who Zach Morris is. I forget I am so young, pretty much a baby. My obstacle sounds like that of a young girl who hasn't faced too much in her life yet. My brother and sister in law lost their first baby, Kinley, when I was in high school and that crushed me. It ripped my heart out and left me bitter and sad. But I don't feel that is my story to write fully, because my brother and his wife have the most hauntingly beautiful and redeeming words to share about my niece and her impact on this world and you should hear that from them. Wow. Talk about a heartbreak. Dailyglimpsesofheaven.blogspot.com

Of course, I have hard times. Times where depression clouded my vision, months on end where one thing after another was yanking me down. Like the last few months, car is unfixable, a family member passed away and I am miles from family, three different jobs in the last year, and I snapped at my husband far too many times to win wife of the year, along with so many disappointments. But, I have been fortunate enough to come from a blessed household with parents who are together and in love (go mom and dad!). I have siblings who love Jesus and are far wiser than me. So, my biggest obstacle for a 24-year-old with a happy home was a breakup I went through in college. After three years, we broke up after being told I wasn't loved for the last year of the relationship. I mean we had looked at rings; this was going to be it! He was my everything. I was crushed, depressed, anxious, couldn't get out of bed or eat, failed college courses because I skipped class, was stone cold to those who loved me, was angry and bitter at God.

For an entire year I was engulfed in darkness. Complete and utter shame about mistakes we had made together. Feeling overwhelmingly not good enough, heart ripped out of my chest, and ignoring a seemingly very distant God. I think there are a lot of experiences that can leave us feeling this way. My momma played a huge role in helping me navigate this time. She spoke into me the verse in Philippians 4:6. "Do not be anxious about anything but in everything... Pray!" I summarized that, but you get it. It still speaks this to me. (I called her just the other day and she still reminds me to pray with this verse.) She always directed me to God, even when I wanted nothing to do with Him. I thought I knew better than Him and would have chosen the boy over Him in a heartbeat, had it come to that. She would suggest things like making lists of things that I was thankful for, and believe me, it was a short list at that point! She said to help others, another thing I was like what the heck, "No". I'm falling apart over here, can't help anyone else. But then I would meet someone even fresher out of a painful breakup and immediately I was drawn to them. I would want to hold them in my arms and hear them and cry with and for them. They were so healing for me, as I hope I was for them. I believe I went through it, not only because God had something better for me, but also to show me how He can work to bring my pain and someone else's together in hopes we could find Him in the embrace. I wasn't alone, and in fact I was very much held and in company with the God of the stars.

I started seeing Him in things again.

Like an extravagantly pretty sunrise, a good iced coffee, in songs like "It is Well With My Soul," and in people with much more grace for me then I deserved. I was a dirty no good rotten friend to my people during this time, and because they were Jesus-loving people, they took me back. I wrote a good blog post about this season in my life and would love for everyone to read it! (I want everyone to read it because well, GOD! He's awesome!) It was written from a real and painfully raw place. God had waited for me while I had pushed him away. I found Him again and this time I was never letting go!

FAITH – Many people struggle with having faith when things around them seem to go awry. What would you advise someone who wants to strengthen their faith?

You know how it's way easier to see where God was and how He was working on the other side of a trial? What if we could believe He was there with the best for us during the trial? That is something I think of every time I feel the weight of this world and sin. If you can train yourself to speak verses of truth and believe that he is in control during the trial, faith proves itself over and over. James 1:6 says "But when you ask, you must believe and not doubt, because the one who doubts is like a wave of the sea, blown and tossed in the wind". That means as doubters we are shakable, unstable, with nothing to ground us. If you have trouble with doubt, ask God to help your unbelief. (Mark 9:24, I believe God, but help my unbelief!) If you're not in some sort of community group with a church or have people pouring into you, I would look for that and cling to women there. I moved away from those I went to for everything, but the good news is, God follows you wherever you go. I found God in community in New Orleans! I'm still building new relationships. Find people who are willing to be vulnerable and real with you. That may begin with you. Everyone is scared to share their shortcomings, but when you share others follow. You've got to have other people. You can't do it alone. Yes, God is all you need. If it was you and no one else on a deserted island, God would be enough, He is enough. He provides us with the desire to be in community, so that we don't have to do life alone. How would we make a difference for His kingdom if we weren't with people?

A few months ago, I heard a sermon that hit me hard. It was during a season where I was trying to go at it alone. Todd, God and I was good! I prayed, read my word, and I felt solid. But I wasn't sharing that with anyone else. The pastor was talking about the body of Christ and I knew about that, so I tuned out. How funny it was when he said some convicting words straight to me, in my face. He said, "Yes the church is the body of Christ. But listen, you can't be connected to the head and not the body." What!? Dang it. I must be friends with people. I must be connected to the body or else we are just a head. Okay God, I hear you. So, I tried to let people in. Although it was far from comfortable at first, I now feel much more alive, cared for, and supported. One Sunday I walked out of service and walked right up to the service desk for childcare to volunteer. That was a bold and rewarding step for me. Read Hebrews 11 where we are shown several faith stories. With faith, we are grounded in God's truth. Next time you go into a trial, think this: "Every time I don't trust God during my trial, He brings me out of it. I wish I had trusted Him the whole time!" Me too, sister, me too.

OVERCOME - How do you structure your time to reflect all the priorities and opportunities God has given you to be a light for him without losing yourself in the process, both personally and professionally?

Wow these questions are awesome because I am forced to really evaluate my time with Jesus. I am a classic example of saying yes to doing all the cool things I am asked. Everything may be a good thing. You may enjoy doing many things. But you have to say no to good things sometimes. If you don't, you will only put half your heart into a bunch of things. You want all your heart in a few things. So, say no to good things! Sometimes, I say, not now, maybe later when I've given the time and space.

When structuring time, ask yourself, "what is important" when it comes to the things I am doing or want to do. My answer is always people. People are important because they're God's best and messiest creation. Sometimes I feel like I come home from a long day's work, and suddenly all the hours are gone. I go to bed and do the same thing over again tomorrow. I don't even know what happened to those evening hours. Did I talk to my husband, paint or read a good book? Or did I stay on my phone and watch Netflix mindlessly until it was time for bed? Don't get me wrong, I love a good Netflix night! We all need those every once and a while, but every night?! I can't, it makes me sad. I realized how un-present I was with my husband, my bible study, etc. I convinced myself, I wouldn't have time or energy to have a deep conversation with anyone until the weekend, so what is the point of trying to be present..." WHAT!? When I had this thought, I threw it out. That's no way to live and love in relationships. USE the hours you have. Even if they are for you and that makes you feel selfish, like, taking a long bath, painting your nails, calling a girlfriend and talking about nothing. Make sure you're treating your mental health just as importantly as your physical health. That isn't selfish. Give yourself time to sit and breathe. At least once a day if not more. I take a little longer bathroom break if I need to have more time for me. No shame.

If you are healthy, your ministry will be healthy. If you have spent time with God this morning, the people you interact with will see Him in you today. If you live in His love; smile at strangers, care for your coworkers, go out of your way to say a kind word, ask for patience, pray through the bad and hard days, He will be seen, and people will wonder. In my side business, I am honest about the time it may take me to finish an order. I strive to have integrity when they've waited longer for a piece of art than I promised. I'll stick a little note in the package, and not charge them the full amount. I share all of this to say, for a very unorganized and messy individual, being present in and prayerful with the hours I have and living a kind and loving life because of God's love...that's the best I got!

OVERCOME - Share with us about a season in your life that God sent you through that changed the course of your life.

Oh Lord. This is another question where I feel like God is snickering along with me. Girl, I am IN the season where God is sending me somewhere that will change the course of my life. In the last few weeks, I left my family, moved out of my house for the first time 1,000 miles away, left my lifelong best friend, got married to a man whom I had never lived in the same state with, left college, and got a big girl job. A Midwest girl in a southern city like New Orleans was a shock. When you are in a completely new place, physically, spiritually, mentally, it is hard to know what God wants you to do in all the areas. In new friendships, it is hard for me to ask for help because I want to do things on my own. In fact, I don't ever like asking for help and I'm sure you can see how that's problematic for life. Plus, I missed my old friends. When I got my first full time job, it was an administrative assistant position and I needed it because my husband was still in school and I was bringing home the bacon. I was an art major crunching numbers; not my thing at all! When Todd couldn't meet my expectations in marriage and I couldn't meet his, I wondered, why is this so hard? God, am I really going to be this snappy, selfish, non-cooking wife our whole marriage? Not to mention someone who cares about how someone else brushes their teeth and then doesn't clean the toothbrush long enough for it to be clean. I care a lot, about that stupid thing.

Speaking of teeth… do I have to keep seeing a dentist for the rest of my life?! Now I must pay for that myself? When I moved, I didn't have my mom scheduling my doctor's appointments anymore. (Anyone still in college or new to adult-ing let me hear you celebrate moms for this reason alone.) In fact, I didn't even have a doctor. Still don't. How do you just get one of those? Lord please, I cannot deal.

I am constantly being changed by God in this season daily. I am forced to be changed, because everything around me has changed. I have learned how to make friends, and that the closest ones are the ones who know Jesus and therefore know the best part about you. I have learned to ask for help and become vulnerable with my new friends. It's been sweet and tender to see into their hearts and watch us fall into deeper friendships as time passes. I have learned that God is the only thing that can satisfy me. I have learned that marriage is beautiful and messy but if Jesus is at the center it flows like sweet honey! I have learned that God may not reveal my purpose in my timing. In fact, He hasn't. I wanted to know a long time ago, but He knows I need to work on being patient.

I was telling my husband that I am not doing enough for His kingdom here and I can't wait to do more. I'm not where I was when I was comfortable. I am not who I was, and I am being changed daily to better serve Him in all I do.

POUR -What three scriptures would you share with someone if they are in a season of transition and need clarity? Also, share why you selected these three scriptures.

One of my favorite verses for a struggling heart in transition is Romans 5:1-5 "Therefore, since we have been justified by faith, we have peace with God through our Lord Jesus Christ. Through him we have also obtained access by faith into this grace in which we stand, and we rejoice in hope of the glory of God. Not only that, but we rejoice in our sufferings, knowing that suffering produces endurance, and endurance produces character, and character produces hope, and hope does not put us to shame, because God's love has been poured into our hearts through the Holy Spirit who has been given to us." Another version says, "Hope does not disappoint." If that isn't a perfect tattoo I don't know what is. I love how this verse comes from a place of pain, but ultimately gives you an awesome redeeming hope. It's a powerful anthem I'll sing when I am just so tired of storms of life.

For you created my inmost being; you knit me together in my mother's womb, I praise you because I am fearfully and wonderfully made; your works are wonderful, I know that full well. My frame was not hidden from you when I was made in the secret place, when I was woven together in the depths of the earth. Your eyes saw my unformed body; all the days ordained for me were written in your book before one of them came to be." Psalm 139:13-16. How intimately did our Father in heaven create us? He wove me together, piece by tiny piece, with His hands, in love. As an artist, I don't know why anyone would spend time on us like this if he didn't care immensely about the process and final product. Now do you see how He intends for us to have a beautiful purpose and redeeming story? If you are fighting for clarity in a season of transition, remember whose you are and how He made you. Ask Him to bring to the light how He knew all your days and what you would be like even before you were born.

Ladies hear this one. 1 Corinthians 10:15 "But by the grace of God I am what I am, and his grace to me was not without effect. No, I worked harder than all of them—yet not I, but the grace of God that was with me." Initially, I recognize the sass in this verse, "I am what I am!" Then I noticed the hard worker with the sass. Truthfully, the most crucial part of this powerful verse is the grace that Paul knows he can't be who he is without God. In the verses before, he even claims he is the least of the apostles, (ok, so what am I?) Yikes. He says he doesn't deserve to be one. He knows it is only by the grace of God that he is worthy enough to preach the Gospel to the nations. As women of God, we should stand tall in who we are because we have been saved by God's grace. In turn we can work hard to run our businesses and ministries while sharing our faith with people.

POUR -What is your favorite scripture, and how has that influenced your role as a woman who works and walks by faith?

My favorite scripture is James 1:2-4. "Count it all joy, my brothers, (and sisters) when you meet trials of various kinds, for you know that the testing of your faith produces steadfastness. And let that steadfastness have its full effect that you may be perfect and complete, lacking in nothing." Would you ever believe I didn't really like this verse the first time I heard it? Sounds easier said than done thing, so don't even say it! But this became MY verse in the season after the breakup. Since I clung to it, so deeply, I think it's just morphed its way into my heart and become my life verse. This is how I break it down for myself. First, count it all joy when you face trials? Why and how do I do that? It's not our instinct at all, but James says count it all joy. The Message says, "Consider it a sheer gift, friends, when tests and challenges come at you from all sides." Oh no, I'm for sure going to run.

But wait, "you know that under pressure, your faith-life is forced into the open and shows its true colors. So, don't try to get out of anything prematurely." I spent 4 years in a season God had me in dealing with depression and loneliness up until now. I've don' t mind a sad season. I know that sounds crazy but stick with me. I learned it's okay to be sad and feel all those emotions that come with being sad. Feelings like pain, heartbreak, loneliness, depression, fear, insecurities, etc. I personally need to feel the very depths of my pain. If I can feel it all, I can give it ALL to Him, and not hold onto any of it. Another thing I don't mind about these seasons is that I recognize my need for Him like I need air to breathe. There are times I am not able to physically breathe because of my emotions, depression, or anxiety. (Side note: there's nothing wrong with seeing a therapist and I take anti-depressants that really have helped me in this season). The only thing that can help is God's existence. I need Jesus like air! And I need to be reminded or I forget.

Trials no longer scare me, they say to me "you're about to be pressed but stick with God." Remember, you will be perfect and complete - lacking nothing! That doesn't mean trials aren't hard! Sure, they are, the hardest, and sometimes I just want answers and I want out. However, this verse is my favorite because it reminds me of all the times I prayed it, what I went through with God, and how I am on the other side now. Please let yourself feel everything. So, you can gain fully with the Lord and come out complete in Him. Allow how you feel in the trials cause you to be vulnerable in your ministry. Remember what it's like to need God like air. Like my momma says, we always do. As women, we need to build each other up and what better reminder that we are worthwhile than this verse. If we can do this part of life together, oh wow, that's a piece of heaven! "Let it do its work so you can become mature and well-developed, not deficient in any way". The Bible says that when you are tried you will come forth as gold! I am hard pressed but not crushed, persecuted not abandoned, struck down but not destroyed. Hard pressed- like a diamond, maybe for a long time it seems. But we are gold, we are diamonds, and we lack nothing because we travel with God. Count it all joy in trials, because His joy is going to be your strength.

Closing Thoughts

As I close out this chapter, I want to leave you with some encouragement. Wherever you are in your walk with Christ, He wants to use you, your gifts, and your story. I pray that your faith-life is strengthened and that you can already see the extravagant love and plan he has for you. Ephesians 3:20-21: "Now to him who is able to do immeasurably more than all we ask or imagine, according to his power that is at work within us, to him be glory in the church and in Christ Jesus throughout all generations, for ever and ever! Amen." It may be a bigger plan then you can ever imagine for yourself, so hold tight to and be complete in Him.

I love you for reading my heart and hope you see some Jesus in it.

Thank you, Becca

TRACY
MORGAN

Tell us a little about yourself.

My name is Tracy Morgan. Yes, like the comedian. Although we look nothing alike, I do find that I'm quite funny sometimes. My name means warrior, fighter, harvester, brave and courageous. I am a fighter, that's for sure. My strength and passion can be overwhelming to some but to others that see and feel my heart become drawn to me. I am a deep thinker and I ask a lot of questions. I'm curious about how life works and how this entire world is connected and intertwined. I love to laugh and when God reveals himself to me, I can't help but smile with deep joy. At times, I cry tears of happiness knowing the depth of love He has for me. I've been married for almost 10 years (in June 2018) to the man of my dreams. I literally did not think he existed! Calan and I have 1 child that I can't wait to share about. I love bright colors and butterflies and the aroma of unadulterated essential oils. I marvel at creation. I stand in awe among crashing waves in the ocean and I'm fascinated that a tiny ant can carry 50 to 100 times its weight! Above all, I am constantly amazed at how intricate our bodies are. Desiring to become a doctor when I was younger, falling deeply in love with learning about the brain and psychology, mixed with health (and life) challenges of my own since I was a very young girl, has brought me to a place where I passionately desire to share what God has shown me regarding health, our bodies, and the blindness we have to what we can accomplish through Him who gives us strength.

Share with us what your business/ministry is and what it does for those that you serve.

It's amazing how I got here. I never had a childhood dream of serving people with essential oils. I didn't wake up one day and have a revelation that I would be supporting others in their health by my nutritional example. I didn't know God would reveal my lack of obedience to His word to help others find freedom in health as well. But I wouldn't trade it for anything. I've always had a heart for people, for others to be the best God has created them to be, to see God's kindness and love through what He gives us daily, to be free from strongholds, and ultimately to find hope and receive healing. I have been called to serve others through health support and life transformation. When you find something that has changed your life for the better, you share it with people. When you find something that God has done or created for you, you MUST share it with people. Therefore, I share and educate others about essential oils. I don't have all the answers, but His word does, and I know that our daily choices are leading us toward death or life, sickness or healing. My ministry is just beginning, and I am ready to continue to serve in a greater way.

DIRECTION - Sometimes people are confused in recognizing and knowing what they are called to do by the Lord. What advice would you share in how one can hear and know what God has called them to do?

Reflect. Look at your past and present. He has brought you through so much and currently has you somewhere to do His will right now. Don't focus so much on the future. Leave that up to Him. Focusing on the future will only leave you discontented with where He has you right now. Journal the questions that you have.

Pray. Wisdom and discernment are needed, especially during this time. James 1:5, "Our God gives wisdom generously".

Read His Word. It clearly tells us what we are called to do as Christians. If we choose to start focusing on those habits, He WILL reveal His will to you. 1 Peter 4.

Now, start walking. Our God is not a God of confusion or disorder (1 Corinthians14:33). When I've been in a state of confusion, it's been due to internal conflict between my flesh and my spirit; conflict created by disobedience driven out of fear, uncertainty, and doubt to what He has already told me to do. I would challenge you to prayerfully assess if this is the type of confusion and conflict you are in or if it's simply a blessing that God has given you choices. Our God loves us so much that He wants to partner with us in our lives. Take that in for a moment. The God of the Universe, the great I AM, without blemish, wants to partner with *us*, who are full of sin, with selfish ways and greedy hearts. Remember, there is nothing you can do, no choice you can make that will thwart God's ultimate plan. If the confusion is due to choices, pray for discernment, seek counsel from others who are chasing after wisdom, and start walking! Sometimes the vision and story God has for you will be revealed by taking one step at a time with Him…like driving in heavy fog. If you stop your car, heavy fog restricts your visibility and you continue to see the same things. Nothing new is revealed. Continue driving and what happens? Your visibility is still restricted but new surroundings are slowly revealed. "Drive" with Him. He'll reveal new surroundings to you and direct your path (Proverbs 3:5-6).

DIRECTION – There are times when someone may struggle with really knowing their gifts and how to use them. How did you know what you were gifted in, and how do you apply that in your life?

For a long time, even as a Christian, I listened to the enemy tell me that I wasn't gifted in anything. If I felt gifted in a certain area, the next thought he placed in my head was "don't be so prideful".

Ooo how ugly our enemy is! If you are a believer of Jesus Christ, believing that he was fully God and raised from the dead to defeat death for all our sin, past, present and future, then the Spirit has gifted you in one way or another to participate in the body of Christ.

I have always felt this deep sense of understanding and seeing others in a way that went past what they were showing, saying, or doing. I honestly took pride in this as something cool that I could "see right through" people and I exalted myself in this. I remember a phone conversation with my dad many years ago when he told me I could be a very blunt person sometimes and I immediately took offense not understanding what he meant. Spiritual gifts come naturally. We don't have to consciously say, "I'm choosing to use my spiritual gift right now". However, since the beginning of time, the devil has been convincing mankind that all things God has given and created are not good, or good enough. Therefore, even though they are natural, we do have to choose whether we will use them in the Spirit or in our flesh.

Out of my curiosity and desire to know my gifts, I began the discovery process. I took many online tests. I read scripture on what the spiritual gifts were. I also read to determine what gifts each disciple had, so I could have examples of how they lived them out. I evaluated my past experiences such as the ones I listed above. I prayed, asking God to reveal them to me, and prayed for confirmation in what I felt He gave me. Once I knew what I was gifted in, I asked God to give me situations to practice using my gifts (in the Spirit) and to grant me grace as I learned. The mistake that I made was thinking that if I was gifted in it, it would always be perfect. Praise God his mercies and compassions are new every day (Lamentations 3:22-23).

DIRECTION - Many people struggle with developing a habit of including God in all that they do. How do you make God a part of your life/business/ministry each day?

While every day isn't perfect or identical, I have become aware of distractions and temptations. These are tools of the enemy and these silly guys will always be there, especially when you're moving closer to God. If developing this habit is a struggle for you, you are not alone! The first thing I must remember is that there is nothing more important to me than including God in all that I do. If you and I share this importance, we must make ourselves hyperaware of the distractions and temptations that the enemy is constantly throwing in our paths. Make note of these and be creative in attacking them head on.

Health is very important to me. I know that if I'm sick, especially if it's a consequence from me giving in to distractions and temptations, I will not be the best vessel for God to work through for serving, loving, and leading. Since I have been called to serve others with health support and life transformation, one of the biggest ways I make God a part of my daily life and ministry is through my health choices. Do you know how often we're making a health choice? Do you realize how many temptations we are faced with in our society of consumerism and the internal distractions we have in our stomachs and minds? Starting my day strong with prayers for strength and discernment are a must. I read scripture to remind myself that the God I am following and trusting, has been tempted in every way we have but never gave in (Hebrews 4:15), and that there will always be a way out of temptations (1 Corinthians 10:13). I also pray for wisdom, love and leadership for the people that God places in my path for me to serve.

Marriage and family are also an area I make sure to include God in. My husband and I attend church and worship together, we pray daily, and we talk about what we're reading in the Word.

FAITH - As a woman of faith, what has been your biggest obstacle or challenge in your faith walk with God, and how did you navigate that successfully?

My health. I realized while preparing and writing for this chapter that I have gone through all 5 stages of grief with my health. I was diagnosed with Hashimoto's disease at the age of 13 and I did not get to the acceptance stage (fully) until the course of my life was changed when I was 30. I went through denial, anger, bargaining, and depression with my diagnosis. Countless doctors' visits, lab tests, medication changes, side effects and symptoms, all wrapped up with fear that this is what life was.

Praise God He wanted to show me something different. When I met my husband, I was introduced to chiropractic and holistic health. Little did I know that would be the beginning of seeing hope. I began working in a chiropractic office a few years later and I gained more knowledge about the body, nutrition, exercise, and sleep than I did in all my schooling it seemed! Then I started looking at my own body, what it had gone through, what choices I was making, and the hope for what could happen. I made it to the bargaining stage at this time and I remember being swayed to believe that if I prayed hard enough and had enough faith that I would be healed! While I do believe that still happens, I also believe that miracles happen for His glory, not ours. I know my God loves me enough to not leave me to continue in my sinful ways. Let's be honest, if He healed me during that time, I would not have made the changes He revealed I needed to make.

During this time though, I was gaining a lot of wisdom on marriage and my mind was focused on being one and being a team and working together. I remember the day when I broke down in repentance but at the same time was jumping for joy inside when the Lord gave me this example to show me what He desired of me. He desired for me to partner with Him in my healing! This was a huge revelation for me! I no longer felt alone in my disease. I no longer had the mindset of, "I do my thing, you do yours". Once I said yes to this, my eyes were opened to far more than I'm allowed to type here but this is where my ministry began.

FAITH – Many people struggle with having faith when things around them seem to go awry. What would you advise someone who wants to strengthen their faith?

The biggest key here is to be proactive. I was reactive for years as I was strengthening my faith; meaning that I typically ran to God only when things seemed to go awry. I know our God hears our cries and answers whether we are proactive or reactive in this but if you're looking to truly strengthen and grow deep in your faith, being reactive will not allow you to grow in this way. Here are a few proactive ways that have helped me strengthen my faith that I would encourage everyone in.

Become a member of a church that is leading, teaching, and living the standards of the Bible.

Join groups and bible studies with people that are following hard after Jesus. Everything used to tell me, "You can do it alone. You just need the formula or steps to make it happen". Don't listen! Don't isolate yourself like I did. I underestimated the importance of including others of faith and overestimated my ability to "do it myself" and "pull myself up by my bootstraps and keep going". Galatians 6:2 says "Carry each other's burdens, and in this way you will fulfill the law of Christ."

Journal. Throw out your invisible rules for journaling and write about anything. It doesn't even have to make sense. It may not seem like this will help strengthen your faith but once you get comfortable writing about anything, start writing out your prayers and the cries of your heart and watch the transformation. Also, it's always fun to go back and look at where you've been, how far you've come, and what God did for you in His love.

Read the Bible. By now, I'm sure you're thinking, "Yeah, yeah. You've already said this", but I really can't say this enough! It's repetitive for a reason. Just as Peter wrote in his second book, "So I will always remind you of these things, even though you know them and are firmly established in the truth you now have. I think it is right to refresh your memory…" (1:12-13a).

The best time to start strengthening your faith is now. Whether it's reactive or proactive, put these steps into action and if you need help, let me know!

OVERCOME - How do you structure your time to reflect all the priorities and opportunities God has given you to be a light for him without losing yourself in the process, both personally and professionally?

Structure does not come easy for this gal here. I must work at this constantly! One thing Calan and I do is meet once a week to review and measure the goals we set at the beginning of the year. We set up 6 distinct categories with health, spiritual and business included in those. We assess how we did the previous week in each category and discuss what we're striving to accomplish in the upcoming week. We also plan our meals and grocery list which makes that process so much easier when we're at the store. It's a great time for us to connect and plan and it is great accountability to keep us on track. I am at my best when I get up at the same time every day and start my day early. We work out in the mornings 2-3x per week which cultivates discipline and spending time in the Word is finally a daily habit for me to set the intention for the day and thank God for all He's done and all He's doing.

In my business, I have learned that those silly distractions I mentioned previously are enemies to the structure I've worked hard to create. One distraction of mine was the easily accessible from anywhere Facebook app, so I needed to delete it off my phone. It forces me to use my computer for Facebook and I've found that I am more aware of the time I spend on my computer on Facebook than I was on my phone. I have gained hours per week to pour into the priorities and opportunities God has given me by doing this.

OVERCOME - Share with us about a season in your life that God sent you through that changed the course of your life.

Calan and I have been married for almost 10 years. While one could say that we are "struggling" with infertility, we fully believe that it will be by His divine timing that children will enter our lives. In fact, one has already entered. In November 2015, we found out we were pregnant but 10 weeks later, our baby was united with the Creator that had woven its little body into creation. This miscarriage changed the course of my life. As you read this, you are probably thinking that this was a cinch for me/us to go through since we are a family of faith. Let me tell you that this was the. most. difficult. season. I have EVER gone through.

At the time we got pregnant, I would've told you that my faith was strong, but it wasn't. I remember driving to work one day and praying the following prayer: "Lord, hi. It's me. I'm sorry I haven't talked to you in a long time and I'm sorry that I haven't even had the desire to. I have made this baby an idol. It's all I think about, it's all I care about, and you know this is not what I want and desire to be as a mom. I don't want to put my children before you! I can't be the best mom that you've called me to be if I am not following you and seeking you daily. I am so sorry Lord. Please forgive me. And please help me not make this baby an idol because you will always be what I desire most, and you are all that matters."

A few days later our baby was in the arms of Jesus. Time to enter anger and resentment and days and weeks of crying and asking "why" into this part of my story. I forced myself to fight through this pain. I am a fighter, remember? I was hashing this out with God once and for all. He was going to know how I felt about Him giving us this amazing gift that we had been praying for, for 7 years, and then just taking it away from us! I journaled constantly. I had Bethel worship playing constantly. I refused to believe the lies that Satan was telling me and made myself seek out truth and write it and pray it even though I didn't "feel" it. No matter how angry I was and how loud I cried and screamed, I knew in the silence of my soul that God wants and has my best in mind. Nearly two weeks went by, out of work and a lot of alone time, but I wasn't done grieving and I wanted to reach acceptance.

I began feeling more and more peace and love come over me and then I heard the Lord tell me "You will have your rainbow baby.

Trust me and my timing." Over the following few months and years important phrases that the Lord has spoken to me have been "This has to happen first", "I haven't forgotten", "It's not time yet", "Remember, it's not about you", and "I'm here". This season not only changed the course of my spiritual health but also my physical and mental health. My eyes were open to much sin in my life as well as the disaster that our country is in (myself included) regarding health. There's so much I want you to see too. My mission is only beginning, and I praise God that this season is a part of my story. To Him be the Glory forever and ever.

POUR -What three scriptures would you share with someone if they are in a season of transition and need clarity? Also, share why you selected these three scriptures.

Psalm 130:5 – "I wait for the Lord, my soul waits, and in his word I put my hope." I selected this verse as a reminder of what to do during this time. While it doesn't seem to show the way for clarity, there is power when we put our hope in the word of the Lord. The hard part is the fight between what we're longing to hear from His Word and allowing our soul to wait on Him to hear what He wants us to hear.

Proverbs 3:5-6 – "Trust in the Lord with all your heart and lean not on your own understanding; in all your ways acknowledge him and he will make your paths straight." In seasons of transition, I have been tempted to rush and decide quickly out of impatience. However, this only led me to lean on my own understanding and not trust the Lord. In our vocabulary, "always" and "never" are commonly used but rarely true so we might be tempted to think "all your heart" and "all your ways" in these verses don't really mean

ALL of them. Friends, this is a promise that's written. If we do these things, He WILL make our paths straight.

Psalm 77 – This entire chapter in all its context is needed for my last one. The author is crying out to the Lord for help. He's questioning the Lord, wondering if He is even there and if God has forgotten His promises. Wow. I can totally relate to this. Sometimes in a season of transition and waiting, it totally feels like God has gone silent, isn't anywhere to be found, and has stopped leading us. There's an immediate shift after the author realizes the questions he is asking, and his thoughts change. He chooses to appeal his own thoughts and to remember, to meditate, and to praise God for all the things He has done and His miracles of long ago. I chose this chapter because sometimes we can get so caught up in not knowing what to do or where to go that we slowly fade to doubt that God is even there still and even cares. Follow this author's example and choose to praise Him for all He has done in history, in His Word, and in your life!

POUR -What is your favorite scripture, and how has that influenced your role as a woman who works and walks by faith?

There is so much richness included in the entire Bible so it's hard to choose one favorite. As a daughter of Eve but fully redeemed by Christ, trusting God's timing and having patience that He has my best in mind is a constant battle of mine. I want things to happen in my time and to fit into my schedule when it's most convenient including being healed from Hashimoto's and getting pregnant. One of my favorite scriptures for this is 2 Peter 3:8-9.

I love how Peter, out of all scripture written, begins verse 8 with "But do not forget this one thing". You think maybe God knew we would constantly forget this next part? "With the Lord a day is like a thousand years, and a thousand years are like a day." Verse 9 is the best part. "The Lord is not slow in keeping his promise, as some understand slowness. He is patient with you, not wanting anyone to perish, but everyone to come to repentance."

You see? Our time is nothing like His! But my flesh and sinful mind tells me that this life is in *my* time and about *me* but that couldn't be farther from the truth. These 2 verses have influenced the way that I trust God and His timing. To know that He is the creator of time, even though I don't fully comprehend verse 8 with my finite mind, takes a huge weight off my shoulders. And then to know that He's after my soul! He doesn't want me to perish so he is patient with me and desires for me to come to repentance of all sin I am holding on to. Also, when God makes a promise, He is faithful to it. It will happen. Period. It doesn't matter when, that's on His timeline. All that matters is, do I trust Him? If so, I must trust all His promises as well, including His timing.

Any closing thoughts?

To all that have lost hope in their health, to all women who fear their family will never grow, to all in times of sickness and disease, I leave you this prayer and encouragement:

I want you to know that your body is a powerful machine. It's the most intricate design that God has created. With that machine comes a powerful mind but that mind is susceptible to taking hold of things that God never designed to be in there; thoughts that have been tainted with lies from the enemy; and fears that strip us away from seeing and knowing God's faithfulness to that design. Through God's breath, your body has the power to heal itself. Through God's plan, your body has the power to multiply and create life inside! Through God's power, His love set you free! I pray right now that you would be set free. Free from fear, from anxiety, from lies that Satan has whispered to you that things are wrong, things are bad. I pray in Jesus' powerful name that you would trust Him and believe that He has made you in His image and to heal from sickness and disease. I pray that as you rest, that you would trust that sickness takes time to heal (sometimes days/weeks) and nothing is wrong with that. I pray that peace would overwhelm you in this time, that you would learn ways to support the temple He has blessed you with, and partner with him in your healing. I ask that God would bless the faithfulness that you have for Him in this time and that He would bless you abundantly. Being uncomfortable with symptoms of sickness is not a bad thing. It means your body is working! It's fighting! It's healing! I'm lifting you in prayer my friend. But I do want you to know...the fear and worry and anxiety is doing way more harm in your body than the sickness your body is fighting is doing right now. Relax...and breathe...and know your body is fine. Let's support your body with oils soon, add prayer with that, let you get some rest and be thankful for sickness (yes, thankful) and you'll see God work with your health just like I have. He IS faithful.

Sowing health together in His name,
Tracy Morgan, 2 Peter 1:3-11

Update: Upon completion of this chapter, God blessed our trust of His timing for a child and the obedience we took with our health. Our rainbow baby is due December 2018! Apparently, this chapter "had to happen first". Praise Him for His everlasting faithfulness!

CHERYL GINNINGS

As a child of a minister, growing up was more difficult for me than most kids. Why? Think back to your childhood. Add to all your experiences the fact that you are also a preacher's kid. Were you ever called a "PK?" I can remember that people seemed to think we were either angels or demons! That is the truth!

One day, I got to go home with a friend from school whose family I had never met before. As soon as her mom opened the door, she said, "So you are the little devil!" I was stunned! She did not know me from Adam! I had just met her-and never saw her again-but her preconceived idea that I was either a great kid or a little devil almost brought me to tears!

Growing up was the most tough because I was left out of a lot of things, as I was a "PK." When people made fun of me on the school bus, I sometimes did not know what they were even talking about because I was so naive!

I grew up in Virginia, but I attended a Christian college in Oklahoma. It was there that I had a great time with people who shared some of the same values I did. Of course, there were those who pushed the limits, but I was such a pleaser that I would not rock the boat trying to break the rules.

I met my husband there, which was great because I really wanted to marry a minister, which he was going to be. We stayed in Oklahoma for his last year of college and then went off to graduate school in Tennessee. I quit school to work and support us, and I enjoyed it (mostly) until the four years were almost over. I was wondering how much longer we would have to wait to have a baby. I had always wanted twins but am I glad God knew better.

We were so poor that we could not even rub two nickels together and we had no credit cards-since women could not have credit in those, days-but we never went broke. I am thankful that was the way it was, because we never had anything we could not pay cash for, which turned out to be a great thing.

We met good friends in our Bible class and spent every other weekend at each other's apartment eating and playing games. We did not think we had much in common with them since my husband was getting his master's in theology as opposed to the husband was in Medical school and his wife, who was a school teacher, but we stayed friends until they passed away a few years ago.

You never know who you will be best friends with but having a desire to live a godly life and wanting to have close friendships with those who also share that passion opened the doorway to our becoming best friends with this couple. Years later, I told my friend that I thought they were a little "stuck up" because she looked that way-this was in the days of "cat glasses" which gave an appearance of haughtiness. I could not have been more wrong.

As the years went by, we kept in touch off and on. We always felt like we were picking up where we left off. After we moved to Kansas, we went back to see them once, and Lisa and I taught a women's Bible class about David and Jonathan. We shared our love for each other and how we both seemed to have so much in common. She was a true blessing of a friend. When she passed away, we drove to Tennessee, so my husband could preside over the funeral.

So many people came by to see the family that the waiting line was five hours. She had impacted the community for years as an English teacher who went above and beyond. Every person who came through the line had the feeling she was their best friend. Only three months later, her husband Jim died, and we have missed them so much. We are still friends with their four children and thankful for them.

You and I never know where our best friends will come from and need to be open about helping one another and those we meet. I guess I have always desired to have Christian friends around me, and I'm thankful that God has blessed me over and over.

God has surrounded me with people I love; and I'm thankful that God blessed me with a sweet husband who has been my best friend. We love the Lord and knew that we wanted to serve Him above all else.

Has it always been easy? Absolutely not! There are stinkers in and out of churches! There are those who love to find a way to pick and find fault. But there are more who love the Lord and His Bride who try their best to serve Him. Even in the first century, there were people with lots of problems. They are not exempt from troubles or causing troubles for others at times. That is the disappointing part of the Lord's work, but isn't that what the Scriptures teach? Second Timothy 3:16-17 says that the Scriptures are good for finding what the problems are in our lives (I'm paraphrasing) and how to correct them, and for correct teaching about how to live a life that is pleasing to God.

Isn't that great that He knew we would need guidance? We do not have to wonder what pleases God. Matthew 7:21 makes it clear that many will believe they are going to Heaven who are not. Only those who do His will are. So, the struggle some of us have is to know what is pleasing to Him, and not to us! As humans, we sometimes get into trouble by focusing on pleasing ourselves, being entertained, or just doing whatever we like and think that pleases God, too.

How do you find out what is pleasing God? It takes a lot of study and a willing heart to be open to change. Remember, while Christ was going up to the mount and everyone was following him, he turned and told them if they did not hate their moms and dads, they were not worthy to follow Him. He did not mean we are to hate our parents, because he tells us to honor them in Ephesians. He just doesn't want us to say, "If it is good enough for mom and dad, it is good enough for Him." You see, many moms and dads do the best they know how, but even that is not according to God's will or God's word.

That is the challenge for us as women to really love the Lord enough to read and study His word and do our very best to bring up children who also love Him. Carving out time for God is a challenge most people have. It is something we must dedicate ourselves to. Teaching others God's will makes us study more, or it should. We will be judged more harshly, James says, if we are teachers because we have people who listen to what we say. That makes our role within a minister's family more challenging, because we must live the way we teach.

It's a sad thing to see many people who are caught in sin who were preachers, teachers, or workers for the Lord and I just wonder what they really believed while they were teaching others. As members of a minister's family, we need to realize that more people watch everything we do to see if we mean what we teach. Oftentimes, they are looking for flaws-and they will find some when they look very hard.

There have been some very tough times in our lives that really challenged us as to whether we were meant to be in a minister's home. At one time we even thought we should see if my husband could get into the Air Force because we had a son with cerebral palsy, and we were not paid well enough to afford medical insurance. That was one of the most challenging times in our lives, but we trusted God.

It seems that there have been some tough times in our lives where we would pray that things would work out the way *we* just knew God wanted them to because we thought we knew what was best for us. We were wrong from time to time. However, when God closed a door on us, within a few months we would see a new challenge open. I always said, "If God closes a door, He will open a window."

You may feel that way, too. We pray for things to work out and they don't. But how many times do we thank God that they did not work out the way we wanted because something else was better for us? We have enjoyed many opportunities that made us grow. It is tough, but the Scriptures teach us to pray all the time. That's not just when we are in a mess! Paul writes that we should pray even when there are bad times, and if he did it, we can, too. Of all the people in the Bible, Paul learned so many lessons the hard way, but he never lost faith in God. He was beaten, shipwrecked, thrown into prison, etc. But always came out blessing God.

One of the greatest lessons I have learned from Paul was that when he was Saul, he would go around throwing people in prison who were Christians, but later found out he was wrong. He said (paraphrasing again), "but I did it in all good conscience." Wow! He admitted that when he was wrong, he still thought he was right. He learned later that he did not do what was right and immediately changed his life and let those hard things he had done in his past be forgiven when he was taught to be baptized.

Another wonderful lesson from his story was when he changed his life, he did not go around being hurt by the guilt of his past. He knew he was forgiven, and he let go of the wrongs he had been forgiven of. I have seen people who were forgiven by God never forgive themselves. How sad! Their shoulders must really be tired carrying all that guilt around.

I have gone through many hard times, but I never struggled for a moment with knowing that God was with me. I did not have to see it at the time, but I have always known that if I am trying to do right and following His will, He will see me through everything. We have truly had some very, very difficult times.

There was a time that my body was giving out because of caring for my special needs' son, a baby, a young daughter, and my mother-in-law, who'd moved in with us when her husband died. I became very sick and ended up in the hospital. The doctors found that I had a bad case of mono, among other things. The doctor called the day after I left the hospital and told me they thought I had lung cancer, but "don't worry about it." He said I was too sick, but he had already spoken with a surgeon. That very night, we called a place that helped children with cerebral palsy, and they let our son come and stay for a while.

I had to be taken care of for six months, and during that period, when our son would come home for a visit, we saw how we could not lift him and care for him all the time. It was one of the darkest times in our lives. I would tell people that old saying, "I want patience, and I want it right now!" I was reminded that James 1 teaches that we learn patience through hardships. I realized that I had been praying for the wrong thing. But I also learned that through all of that, the challenges we have will build our character, and that is something that is necessary for our growth.

There have been so many challenges in our lives with a special needs son; including all the care he needs, the equipment, the medical attention, etc., that it brought us to our knees a lot. People are always reminding me of the Scripture that God won't give us more than we can handle, but I took that wrong. I thought that if things were too hard, or if *I thought* they were, then it meant that I would have to continue to care for our son only in our home. That passage does not mean that. I have not physically been able to handle all he needs for a long time. Does that mean that I am not following God? Am I still trying to meet all his needs, even if he is not in my personal care 24/7?

I learned years ago what it was like to see people struggle when they could not physically take care of their parents in their own home. There is a lot of guilt associated with it. However, this passage does not imply that. We are looking after family, even if we are not personally doing it. If we are keeping up with their needs, trying to see about them, and making sure they are well cared for and have their needs met, we are lovingly caring in the way we can.

Because of the caring for so many in our family throughout all our lives, I've become more sympathetic toward people with special needs children, those with any disabilities, our wounded warriors, and our parents. I see how we need to stand and speak up for those who cannot do so for themselves.

My heart aches to see children being made fun of or bullied because of some disability they have. I speak up for them, and I love challenging those who might not see their needs as personal. I teach others how to care for one another in a deeper way than I would have if I had not experienced having my son and a father who became an invalid after a surgery that went wrong.

I share the Scriptures with people who want to know where God is when they are going through transitions that are often very painful. I know that God is where He was when His only beloved son was hanging on the cross. He loved His Son so much, but He loved us too. He is a just and merciful God who allowed His only Son, who was perfect and did not deserve to die, to take our place so that we could be saved. This is a hard thought to understand, except to know Jesus was perfect and we are not. The only way we could go to Heaven is if Jesus took our place and paid the price of our Salvation.

I look back at Acts 2 on the day of Pentecost. Peter was preaching to the very people who had crucified Christ! Imagine! There are the very people who crucified Christ, and Peter tells them what they did! They had not realized until then that Christ was truly the Son of God. They were looking for an earthly king and did not believe Jesus was God's Son. When they heard those words and found out they were responsible, they wanted to know immediately what to do to be saved.

Peter told them they had to repent and be baptized, because that was the only way they could have their sins washed away and be saved. That was the first time that people were able to have the forgiveness of sins under the New Law. Under the Old law, they had to have a priest make sacrifices for them. But under the new law, it was so much better and easier to repent of sins and have them washed away with baptism to be saved. Isn't it grand that we live under the New Law? No more animal sacrifices. No more of the many laws that the people of God under the old covenant lived under. God is so good!

I love to read the book of Philippians which teaches us to have the attitude that Christ had. He was willing to obey His Father in heaven, even to his death on the cross. We are to have the same attitude. To live for Christ is to pave the way to going to heaven. That is my goal. I want to live with God on high and take as many as possible with me. I don't deserve it, but God has made a way possible for me to have my sins washed away. What more could I ask?

There are so many people that I have been with during their challenging times. I pray for those who are struggling and do not realize that God loves them, but because He made us independent people with the power to choose to love Him or not, we must realize that many of our own hardships are because we make wrong choices out of wanting to please ourselves instead of Him. We must assume our personal responsibility to obey God to be in Heaven with Him someday. I love sharing that message with others. God truly loves us, even when we are having a very difficult time.

If you want to reach out and talk to me about anything I have shared, please do. I would love to help you through your tough times.

CHRISTAN BARNETT

28Bold is a 501c3 approved non-profit that provides water relief on the continent of Africa. We partner will local churches and use the water relief not only as a practical means to meet a need, but also as an outreach tool to tell others about the love of Jesus. 28Bold began after I went to South Africa on a short-term mission trip with my local church. I had always dreamed of going to Africa, so at the time I thought this was a bucket list item that I would be able to check off my list. However, it became much more than that and my eyes and heart were open to the needs far from my homeland. I remember at one point standing on the ground in Africa thinking "I have a choice- I can go home and act like this didn't happen and feel more comfortable or I can go home and make a difference." I chose to go home and make a difference and 28Bold was birthed.

Knowing God's plan for your life can be confusing and daunting, however, God created us each uniquely and with unique gifts and talents. He placed passions and interests in us for a reason and that reason is to use them to glorify Him. Practically, look at your interests. How can you use them for Him? It does not necessarily have to be profitable or a fulltime job; it could be as simple as blogging or prayer. At the end of it all God's will is whatever you can use to glorify Him and bring the lost to Christ.

While there are many spiritual giftings and talent guides that exist and can be helpful, simple conversations with those closest to you can help you discover your gifts and talents. Sometimes what we are good at comes so naturally that we don't even see it. Your friends and family can help you explore these and recognize them for what they are!

God is a part of what I do every day by staying in prayer and any time there is a decision to be made I ask for wisdom. Many times, if

I think about what Jesus would do or imagine how God would want me to respond; the answer becomes very clear. In business I remind myself that it all comes back to making our creator famous. How can I make Him known? How can I make this business decision in an ethical, holy manner? When Christ is the focus decisions can easily be made! More practically, I am part of two different daily group texts- one that is made of close friends and the other of my small group. These ladies encourage me, and we are real with one another. Having a daily text thread gives me close access to godly women that want to see me be more like Him. I have made many parenting and business decisions with the guidance of these ladies and they are quick to remind me that in Christ, I am ENOUGH.

The biggest obstacle in my faith became my greatest moment of overcoming. At 21 I found out I was pregnant as an unwed college student at a Christian private school. The relationship I was in was abusive and I was very disconnected from friends and family. I was asked to leave the school. So, I moved back home with no job, no money and no hope. I was depressed, suicidal and dangerously isolated-feeling very rejected by the community I thought was grace giving. I vividly remember telling God "you have to save me from this. I'm in too deep. I don't see a way out." I opened my Bible and found the scripture in Isaiah 48 that says, "though the mountains be shaken, and the earth be removed, my love for you will never end." Reading that scripture that day was the catalyst for allowing God in my life in a deeper way. Now it has been more than 13 years and I can honestly say God was and has been more faithful, kind and generous with His love than I ever knew possible. When I turned it over to him He blew my mind with how He could restore my life, which was so broken. Additionally, walking through such a dark time has given me a stamina to endure tough times. God has also opened so many doors for me to speak into other women's' lives in similar situations.

When I struggle to have faith I really take it back to the basics I know- reading the word, staying in the fellowship of believers and listening to worship music. Additionally, it's important to *let someone know*. Satan has a tricky way of isolating us when we are vulnerable, making us that much more vulnerable. When I am struggling with my faith my instinct is to pull back, isolate, disconnect. Christ created the church for support, he said the church is like a doctor, he came to heal the sick; he did not come for the healthy. It's also helpful to take a little stock of what I am taking in each day. Music, television, people, work, all these elements of our lives make deposits. We have control over what we allow in our lives. Choosing to be surrounded by positivity, faith-filled messages and people are going to help support our faith.

The season that changed the course of my life the most was probably the season as an unwed mother. I remember praying such simple prayers, some out of sheer desperation and some out of ignorance. My child had a lot of health problems, I was 21 and in school and working full time. Looking back, I have no idea how I got through, but by the grace of God. There are decisions today that I made in that season that directly impact my everyday life. Everyone's story can look different, but at the time I was begging the birth father to be part of our child's life. I was desperate to make a family, even if it meant it didn't quite look like the traditional unit. Bio dad was inconsistent at best. I remember thinking "he's an adult just like me. He can choose to parent just like I did, but he's not." It dawned on me that no healthy relationship should have one person begging for attention. A healthy relationship is balanced. I stopped begging him and he stopped coming around. Around that time, I told

God that I was fine if it was just He, my child and me for the rest of my life, but I wouldn't settle to be tolerated, I wanted to be celebrated. Not only did that season teach me so much independence at an early age, but it also taught me dependence on Christ. It was just a few months later that I began dating the man who would ultimately be my husband and adopt my fatherless son. I truly believe our seasons were aligned because of our individual dependence on our Savior.

DANA GAILEY

Tell us a little about yourself.

I am a home school grandmother. I was a little girl who was a struggling student yet have found myself in classrooms loving children for decades. God picked me up and called me His own when I was twenty-five, and the next year I embarked upon the sweetest job of my life as momma. I have been married to Don Gailey for twenty-six years, and together we have seven children and nineteen grandchildren.

Jesus is my best friend. I love my family, hot baths, sunshine, storms, seasons, going barefoot, pretty shoes, beautiful flowers, people-time, down-time, prayer, and God's beautiful Word. In children and animals, I see the goodness of God - that He would create such marvels.

Share with us what your business/ministry is and what it does for those you serve.

Life is ministry. I continue to learn that in every face in front of me, I am seeking, not always succeeding, but seeking to live in such way that the aroma of Christ is left behind. Though I still get in His way at times, my prayer is that my ministry is the people God places in my path.

Therefore, my husband is my ministry. When I was raising little boys, they were my ministry. As a classroom teacher, my students were my ministry. And now my friends, adult children, step children, and grandchildren are my ministry. In teaching women, the Bible and what God says in His word and in writing for women who read my books, they are my ministry.

My neighbors, the teenager bagging my groceries at Kroger, or the young lady checking me out at Hobby Lobby are my ministry. The Lord has me here to love the face in front of me…whoever that might be. My hope is that through my life I am ministering the gospel of Christ and pointing those I serve to Jesus.

DIRECTION - Sometimes people are confused in recognizing and knowing what they are called to do by the Lord. What advice would you share in how one can hear and know what God has called them to do?

For some, their calling is apparent early in their lives, but for most, certainly for me, I wasn't sure how God would use me early on. He has given us strengths, weaknesses, passions, loves, likes, and dislikes. Our strengths come naturally to us and are relatively easy. Yet our weaknesses are as much direction from God as our strengths. God uses both to get us where He wants us to be to do the work He has called us to do.

So, we trust Him to get us there. The whole idea of trusting God is to simply believe what He says is true. He has told us that He so loved the world that He gave His Son to die for us to give us eternal life. His plans are good for us and not for evil, to give us hope and a future. He is working all things for our good as He is changing us into the likeness of Jesus. Finally, He is doing all this with great purpose, so we will touch our world with His love.

The question is, "Do I believe that?" Do I live like I believe that?

Though it is scary to open ourselves up to trust God completely, it is in that trust place that He can fill us up with His love and lead us. The greatest battle is believing that God loves us that much, so much in fact, that He will open and close doors in front of us as we trust Him.

First, we choose to trust God. Then we do the next thing. Elisabeth Elliot, a 20th century missionary who trusted in Jesus through every season of life no matter what it brought her way, taught me this simple but profound lesson.

Just do the next thing!

When you wonder if you are walking in the Lord's will for your life, just do the next thing He puts in front of you and do it the very best of your ability.

Some time ago, after thirty years as an educator, I stepped away from the classroom, disheartened, weary, and worn out. At almost 60 years old, I felt 'used up.' Though the Lord gave me a couple of years to recover from decades of neglecting myself, 'used up' was not what He had in mind for me. My life continues to be full speed ahead... just doing the next thing He gives me to do.

DIRECTION – There are times when someone may struggle with really knowing their gifts and how to use them. How did you know what you were gifted in, and how do you apply that in your life?

During my teaching and child rearing years I would write in the late hours of the night and then feel guilty because I knew I should have been in bed. I didn't know then that after I was 65 years old, I would have two books in print with more to come. I also did not know that I would spend a few eternally gratifying years homeschooling one of my granddaughters. These have been my most recent 'next things.'

I believe I am gifted in loving and teaching children and women and have learned through the years to impart knowledge and teach them that Jesus loves them.

How did God get me to that place? He nudged me toward elementary education as a college major because it required the least math for graduation. I looked over those degree plans, and the choice was easy! God uses both our gifts and struggles for His glory, and I found this gift of teaching through one of my weaknesses not a strength.

Many people struggle with developing a habit of including God in all that they do. How do you make God a part of your life/business/ministry each day?

I knew from the time I was saved that Jesus was with me … knew my every thought, every word I uttered, in my dreams, in every encounter. That should have been enough to include Him in it all, right? That should be enough not to compartmentalize Him his allotted quiet time, prayer time, and church time. But often it is not.

So, He offered me an opportunity to get to know Him intimately. Shortly after I came to know Jesus as my Lord and Savior, I found myself (rather Jesus and me) raising three little boys. All I had ever wanted to be was a momma. I loved being a mother to my sons more than anything else in this life. But teaching full time and raising them without a daddy in the home with none of my family living near was very difficult. I describe these as the most difficult, most wonderful years of my life.

I was so sleep deprived that at times when I lined my students up to go to the restroom I would lean against the wall and fall asleep (no kidding). I was so tired when I laid in my bed at night that if an intruder had come in and disturbed my sleep, I believe I would have beaten him up myself! It was lights out early in our house when I would sit in the hall and sing praises to God, so my boys could fall asleep with peaceful hearts. Often there was not enough money to make it to the end of the month, yet somehow, we always made it to the end of the month. Those were hard days, but through this time I began to really know my Jesus.

It was my desperation, my pain, my hopeless need for Him to give me strength to get through each exhausting and overwhelming day and night that deepened my relationship with Him. I had nowhere else to go. It was then that I began to learn God's sweet words and His promises and His precepts for living. In my mind - right out loud - through the day and night - just God and me - still the safest and sweetest place for me.

FAITH - As a woman of faith, what has been your biggest obstacle or challenge in your faith walk with God, and how did you navigate that successfully?

My biggest challenge is losing Mary in my Martha world! Do you remember the picture in the gospels of Mary at the feet of Jesus and her sister, Martha, hustling around to get a meal on the table for a house full of guests? I love to sit at the feet of Jesus. I knew that forty years ago, and it is so today. My relationship with my Lord is personal. For it to stay personal though, I must STOP, pour my heart out to Him, open His beautiful Words, and ask Him to, "Speak to me Father…Show me, Lord."

I desperately need to be still to know He is God, and I am not. Yet the work, work, work of a woman's world makes me a Martha all too often. When I have not spent time at the feet of Jesus and taken into my heart His sweet words, I lose Mary. When I lose Mary, I am more easily affected by other's sin, allowing it to rob me of my joy instead of praying for the person and letting it go. When I lose Mary, I am more likely to let my thoughts be selfish or dark instead of taking them captive to the obedience of Christ. When I lose Mary, I carry the load of my life instead of releasing that burden each day, sometimes each hour, to the Lord.

Jesus said, "Come to Me, all *you* who labor and are heavy laden, and I will give you rest. Take My yoke upon you and learn from Me, for I am gentle and lowly in heart, and you will find rest for your souls (Matthew 11:28-29 (NKJV). When I STOP and talk to my Father and read His Words, taking the time to lay my burdens down, He does give me rest for my soul.

FAITH – Many people struggle with having faith when things around them seem to go awry. What would you advise someone who wants to strengthen their faith?

Faith for me is simply believing what God says is true through the sunny days and seasons AND the storms. This is simple but not easy. It means I choose to believe that He loves me with an eternal love. One circumstance after another, I decide if I am going to trust that God is in the midst.

To trust someone, I must get to know them. I get to know them by spending time with them. So, I read His words to know what He says. Then if He tells me to do something, I need to do it. Unconfessed sin hinders my hearing from God. So, if He convicts me of sin, I need to repent to keep the lines of communication open between us.

I need constant communion with my Father so that when those evil days come, and they will, I will be grounded in the truth. This is not easy in the heat of the battle, so I must to stay close to Him knowing He hears my prayers and answers them. At times I cry out, "How long, Lord? How long?" as I intercede for those who are broken, abused, or have great sorrow.

I know though, that much of my faith walk is waiting. It is waiting on God to do what He has in mind. It is not pushing ahead like Abraham and Sarah of the Bible who sidetracked the blessings of God instead of waiting on His plan to unfold. I have learned that He is faithful, and there is sweetness in waiting on His perfect timing, or His emphatic 'Yes' or 'No' in answer to my prayer.

Do I get weary at times? Yes.

Does God see me through? Yes.

Is He ever faithful? He is eternally faithful.

OVERCOME - How do you structure your time to reflect all the priorities and opportunities God has given you to be a light for him without losing yourself in the process, both personally and professionally?

I am a left brain sanguine blond lady, and even now if I get too many balls in the air, I can be overwhelmed. But I am not out to lunch as much as I used to be. Why? Because this faith walk changes us, sanctifies us, makes us more like Jesus as we allow Him to empty us of ourselves and fill us with Himself.

On a practical level, I use a daily planner and depend upon lists to set priorities and stay on top of my days. You may use notes on iPhone, iPad etc. to keep everything in one place: calendar of events, grocery lists, engagements, thank you lists, etc. When there is too much for one day, I ask the Lord to show me what I must do and what can wait for another day. Planners or lists both remind me what needs to be done and encourages me of what I have accomplished. They are tools to take the swirling lists out of my mind and get them onto paper. They serve to bless me, not to stress me and help me establish priorities.

My greatest obstacle to structuring my time to reflect my priorities though, is wasting time. I could watch the Food Network, Fixer Upper, and old movies all day. Facebook, texting, twitter etc. serve as wonderful ways to reach out, stay in touch with, and minister to people. But when I find myself watching TV, or on my computer, iPad or iPhone too much, I must ask myself, *"Am I wasting God's time?"*. I am not promised tomorrow and need to remind myself daily to seize the day the Lord has given me.

Even as a grandmother, I need to turn those devices off and turn my face and heart to God's work…the people in front of me. I can watch a little TV, communicate and check out things on the internet, and read some books. But I must first read my Bible and pray so that I might have a bit more of the aroma of Christ for the lives I touch.

I have another problem as well. I love to do everything! I would love to be on every mission trip, at every conference, cooking for every shut in, sharing a cup of coffee and the gospel with all my neighbors, ministering to the homeless in our city, volunteering at orphanages, and on and on. You may feel this way, as well.

Through trial and error, and great frustration at trying to do too much, I finally learned a wonderful lesson from my husband, the freedom to simply say 'no.' I have not conquered the I-want-to-do-everything completely but doing better all the time. I am even learning to say no without feeling guilty. Though we might want to do many things, it is ok to say no.

Saying no helps me to take better care of my number one priority, my family. Whether I work 8 to 10 hours a day or not, my Full-time job is still when I come home to my precious family. My children, not my career is all that will be left behind when I am gone. The demands of raising a family are just one season of my life. A 'no' in this season can be 'yes' in the next. It is ok to say 'no'.

OVERCOME - Share with us about a season in your life that God sent you through that changed the course of your life.

Teaching has filled my adult life . . . who I was . . . my identity. There was a time though, when the circumstances in which I found myself made me feel like a failure, like I never had been nor could ever be a good teacher. I emptied my classroom and in sadness and hurt threw away most of the teaching aids I had accumulated through the years. That sense of failure can devastate us, and I was devastated for a while. Though my heart was broken, God used it to get me to the next thing. And if I had not made that change, none of what He is doing through me now would have occurred. God was right there with me…He was in it. My teaching days were not over. He used those hurtful circumstances not only to humble me and teach me, but to get me to the next thing He had for me to do.

POUR -What three scriptures would you share with someone if they are in a season of transition and in need of clarity? Also, share why you selected these three scriptures.

"I have been crucified with Christ and I no longer live but Christ lives in me. The life I live in the body, I live by faith in the Son of God who loved me and gave Himself for me" (Gal. 2:20).

This is who God says we are no matter what our circumstances or what others might say about us. Faith is believing what God says is true!

"And we know that in all things God works for the good to those who love Him, and have been called according to His purpose. For those He foreknew He also predestined to be conformed into the image of His Son" (Roman 8:28,29).

God says He will work it ALL for good. That's crazy, right? But He has promised that He won't waste a thing, not one heart ache, not one treachery or hopeless situation. At our most hopeless, we can remember this promise and ask God to help us believe as we wait to see what He will do with our 'all things'. He is in fact using these things to usher us into that next place.

"Be still and know that I am God" (Psalm 46:10).

I STOP my doing and sit at the feet of Jesus. And when I rise I have more of His perspective of this hurting world and more of His love in my heart.

Just do it!

POUR -What is your favorite scripture, and how has that influenced your role as a woman who works and walks by faith?

My favorite scripture was chosen by one of my last fifth grade classes and printed on our bright yellow t-shirts for field day on the last day of school. My granddaughter illustrated it on a pretty poster which hangs in our home. It is Acts 20:24. "I consider my life worth nothing to me, if only I may finish the race and complete the task The Lord Jesus has given me." It reminds me to seek to live each day as though it might be my last. So, if this were my last day:

- Have I let regrets of yesterday or worries over tomorrow rob me of today?
- Have I allowed God to set me free by forgiving any who have sinned against me?
- Have I enjoyed being God's child?
- Have I loved the people He has given me to love?
- Have I made peace where peace can be made?
- Have I let go of those things I cannot and should not control?
- Have I left the aroma of Christ behind?

Make it so, Father. Make us the women of God you have called us to be. Open the eyes of our hearts so we can see our world with your eyes of love. Give us strength when we are weak. Give us courage when we are discouraged. Give us Your joy. Help us lay our burdens at your feet, to take our crazy thoughts captive, to believe who You are, and who we are because of the cross. In Jesus' name, Amen

ELZABETH MATA

Tell us a little about yourself.

I grew up in a small private school and community, raised by my loving mother and father, Gerri and Randy Godsey along with my amazing little sister, Amy Godsey. She and I are four and a half years apart. When my family needed us to change to public schools beginning my freshman year of high school I was not able to transition well like my little sister did. I became terrified, angry and lost in a perpetual downward spiral. Clinging to anyone who may accept me or make me feel loved. I began a dangerous and painful journey and I was a slave to the fear of rejection, people pleasing, feeling unworthy; desperate to feel accepted, loved and enough.

I lost out on many opportunities during and after those adolescent years which would impact the course of my future. I followed dangerous people into reckless living and relationships until I was 22; when I married a man, who looked almost perfect on paper, but was tragically addicted to prescription medication that contributed to him physically and mentally abusing me. This resulted in the marriage ending after just 1 year. About two years later I met Daniel, the man I would marry 7 years later and am building a life and family with today by God's grace. Our relationship saw many valleys and roadblocks due to the tumultuous life I had created while running far from God all those years. My former life had me a slave to emotional trauma and pain, insecurity, shame, fear, and lack of feeling worthy or accepted by anyone.

By God's grace and protection over my life, I was never seriously or permanently injured in any way from my previous life. I feel as if by miracle. God had bigger plans for my life, just as he has for yours beyond your current circumstances. I lived to see through the storms. In 2015, I put my faith in our Savior Jesus

Christ. It was then that God began to transform me from the inside out. It took intensive work with women of faith and a lot of time, self-honesty and trust in God to bring me to the place of recovery today from the darker years of my former life. It takes constant reliance on God and my sweet community of sisters in Christ locking arms in all of life's ups and downs. My family, mother and father never gave up hope and always treated me with acceptance, love and respect through all the darkest years which modeled God's love, and today in Christ, I take victory over the flesh which once ruled me.

Daniel and I were married March 18th, 2016, I graduated from the University of Texas at El Paso that May, I was celebrating 5 years with the same company, and my life was completely turning around since surrendering my life to God and putting my faith in Christ. That winter of 2016 and subsequent spring, to our great sadness, Daniel and I lost two pregnancies, one after the other. This time was a serious test of faith and trust in God. But our prayers are being answered today as we are expecting our first child this September 2018, and we are so thankful and hopeful.

Through a ministry I serve with called Noteworthy, I have met incredible and strong women who have found God during their time in prison. I am hopeful and thankful they are becoming the beautiful instruments God intended. He can transform out of life's darkest corners and seemingly hopeless times, as in my own life, when we fully surrender and become fully dependent through trust in God, His sovereignty, power, goodness and love. I serve as a caretaker within own my family as well. Serving my family as my main form of work brings me the greatest joy and is where God has called me currently. Alongside this, I work independently as a certified signing agent notary for the real estate industry, and I was recently accepted into a graduate school program for a Master of Science in Clinical Counseling with an emphasis in Christian Counseling. I will be taking online classes while staying at home with our baby for the first few years of her life, and I am so thankful my dreams are coming true. It's a blessing to continue on mission at home with my family while furthering my education within the area of my spiritual gifts so I can serve others in need of mental and spiritual guidance.

I'm passionate about letting others know what God has done in my life. Considering how far I ran from God to surrendering all to Him and trusting fully in what Christ did for us on the cross, assured of where my future lies eternally. The freedom I have in Christ today is my greatest testimony to God's great power, love and grace.

Today I don't have to find my identity in what others think of me or what the world tells me I should be, but instead I root my identity in Christ and seek to know God by following Christ. This alone has given me lasting joy and freedom. Feeling the power of God transforming me, my life, and using me to reach others the more I seek His will, worship, and just TRUST him through the vagaries and storms of life.

God never stops chasing you. He loves you and he is calling you back home every time you drift away or run the other direction. I know this to be true because it's my story. I was the runaway, and he found me right where I was, broken and covered in the dirt I had created. God works best though brokenness and through the worst of storms when His children surrender to Him, stop running, and come home to our good, good Father. He is calling us back home with open arms always, every time we get off path or become lost. Whatever you may be facing in your life, or if you feel you've gone too far to come back home, just turn around right now and ask Jesus, the good Shepherd to take your hand. God loves you and accepts you right where you are, and Jesus WILL take you home.

DIRECTION – Sometimes people are confused in recognizing and knowing what they are called to do by the Lord. What advice would you share in how one can hear and know what God has called them to do?

I know I have struggled, in the past and from time to time, with discerning or obeying what it is that God is calling me to do through different seasons life is bringing me through. I have found it helpful to write down on paper (because I'm a visual learner and processor) in one column, what it is that "I" want or desire, and then in another column, I write what I think God is calling me to do, better yet, His will--not mine. I study the two columns and write down how my desires conflict or are in line with what I think God is calling me to do.

This process has helped me identify and uncover fears, doubts, and insecurities I may have about being obedient to the gentle, and sometimes not so gentle nudges God gives me to move in or away from a certain direction. Then I pray. I ask others to pray alongside me that God guides, strengthens and equips me to overcome my limitations and fears. I remind myself of a couple of truths about our Father: God equips the unequipped who are obedient to his calling in their life. I am an imperfect human and therefore I need to have compassion and patience for my true feelings, emotions, actions, or non-actions. I allow myself to acknowledge these emotions and establish my trust that God will equip me to do whatever it is he has called me to do. I must minimize my ego and self-focus, and try to humble myself to the calling, knowing God will work through me, a vessel and instrument. I can honor Him by saying YES and stepping up to the plate in faith, with readiness and humility.

Fear and comfort are the two biggest emotional/psychological antigens I've identified in myself which have prevented or delayed a response to God's calling in life. But God chases the runaways and those He has called to fulfil his work. He is calling everyone to accept Christ's sacrifice and trust and surrender their life to Him, to be reconciled to Him, for everlasting peace and life. We must be ready and put away all fear, trusting God will equip the unequipped and complete the incomplete in us.

We can learn from the story of Jonah when we recognize the storm in our lives that results when we run from what God is calling us to do. God doesn't seek to punish us but rather mold us into his image, bless us, and give us true life. He wants to give us another chance to STOP running from Him and turn and trust Him and say, "I surrender." He will equip you, trust Him. As in the story of Jonah, Jonah did not want to follow God's call for him to share God's message to the people of Nineveh, but God chased Jonah when he ran, and didn't give up on him in his disobedience. He had boundless love and chased Jonah. God provided a storm for his chosen Jonah so that he would STOP RUNNING. He gave him another opportunity to call out to God in desperation and trust; to relay on God to do the work he was called to do. Given another opportunity to follow God's calling for his life, and by Jonah's obedience, now God's will be fulfilled, just as it can be in our life.

I can see how I too can be disobedient for various reasons like Jonah but am reminded by stories such as this that a storm can come from disobeying God's call on my life to create a chance for me to stop running and call out to and turn to God for help. This storm can be a big ol' interruption saying: "HERE'S YOUR SECOND CHANCE! LEAN ON ME, I AM YOUR GOD, AND I WILL PROTECT YOU. I WILL EQUIP YOU AND FULFILL MY WILL THROUGH YOUR DECISION TO TRUST ME, AND BE OBEDIENT, dear daughter. God uses humans--frail, flawed, broken, stubborn, and disobedient humans to do his work. That seems amazing to me that His power is made great in our weakness (2 Corinthians 12:9) when we can put ourselves aside and step into faith and trust God to complete His work though us; when we are obedient and patient despite our frailty and sufferings.

DIRECTION – There are times when someone may struggle with really knowing their gifts and how to use them. How did you know what you were gifted in, and how do you apply that in your life?

This one is a short answer for me. I ask others who I trust and know me well and try to be patient for God to reveal guidance. The hardest thing for me in doing this is mustering up the courage to humble myself, let go of ego or pride and just go for it.

Then ask several people in my life who know me well, whom I trust have my best interest and who I believe will give me an honest answer; *"What do you perceive are my strengths and my weaknesses?'* Restraining myself from trying to force my own assumptions without asking other's insight or waiting on God's timing and direction has been challenging, but that is where patience is paramount.

A sweet sister in Christ helped me realize that some of my gifts are teaching and explaining things to others, as well as listening with patience through kindness and empathy. I have vacillated between whether I wanted to teach as a profession or not because I couldn't pinpoint what age group I was comfortable teaching or whether I even wanted to teach in a traditional sense. But it doesn't always have to be black or white. I tend to want to put things in tidy, well defined little boxes to help me feel comfortable or in control, but I'm learning that God will use our gifts in ways that may be unconventional, seem random chance to us or out of left field.

At the right moment or time for his work to be fulfilled he will call us to apply our gift(s). We just need to identify them and be ready when God calls on us to use them.

DIRECTION - Many people struggle with developing a habit of including God in all that they do. How do you make God a part of your life/business/ministry each day?

Making God a part of my life and mission each day depends on me staying plugged-in to Him. A great illustration has been made during a church service where I belong. They used a cell phone; an example of *us,* and its charger; an example of staying connected to *God through prayer, quiet time, worship, etc.;* to make the point that without being consistently at different points during the day connected through its charger to the power source of life- God, the cell phone (us)will die out or loose life, literally disconnecting us from others who are trying to reach us, (God's purpose and best for us). The same as when we don't connect with God for periods of time daily, we eventually lose touch with that which gives true life, or it dims out and we find ourselves having a "more of me, less of God and others mentality; it's our human nature to be selfish, and defiant to give up our control to God. Paradoxically, our selfishness leads to the very things we are selfishly trying to avoid: misery, pain, loneliness, shame, unfulfillment, fear of missing out.

The scripture that helps me see this clearer is John 15:5, "I am the vine you are the branches. Whoever abides in me and I in Him, He it is that bears much fruit, for apart from me you can do nothing." Jesus used the vine and branches illustration to show us that if we are *not* connected to Him, we wither away and die. He is the vine of life, we are the branches to bear fruit; end of story. We achieve this by plugging into Him as often as possible, daily.

Make the effort to stay connected. Know that we will spiritually die out eventually and miss God's best for us if we don't. We will miss out on opportunities to serve others, a divine appointment to do God's work, an opportunity to deepen our relationship with God, or miss out on growing deeper spiritually that day; if we don't plug into God daily, consistently and for long enough.

Plugging into God for me can look like quiet time in the morning and or evening, prayer throughout the day, just talking to God about my thoughts, fears, questions or petitions in a childlike honest way, or just listening to worship music or a radio show with a pastor teaching while I'm driving. Hey, honestly It may look like after the entire day has gone by and I realize I'm running on empty from not plugging into God, I just talk to God right where I am; be it in the shower- wherever. There are days like this. The gamechanger has been to just plug in and stop wrestling with the guilt of not devoting more time during the day to just be with God. We can't go backwards, but we can choose our next step more wisely. "*This moment (day) is the first moment (day) of the rest your life*"- a wonderful teacher, Joe Sekin, my Grandpa, teaches all his children and grandchildren this mantra in addition to his beautiful poetic work on Love, "Love is the foundation of the soul. Love is self-respect. Love is honesty. Love is the inspiration of the mind." -and I stand by it.

FAITH - As a woman of faith, what has been your biggest obstacle or challenge in your faith walk with God, and how did you navigate that successfully?

My biggest challenge in my faith journey with God so far in my life has been during the devastating season of my two pregnancy losses back to back. My husband and I were just recovering from a surprise pregnancy when we found out it was ectopic resulting in emergency surgery. Then just two hopeful months later we conceived again. Each sonogram revealed a growing uterus and embryo with no heartbeat. My body had missed miscarrying and I would have to undergo two procedures to remove the pregnancy at roughly 9 weeks pregnant.

I was heartbroken and devastated; I grew angry and resentful. I began to torment myself with comparing to others who had hurt me in the past and dwell on their blessings of children and recount the past hurts. It was a confusing and dark time because I had been going through an incredible period of spiritual growth and change, but this was a shot to my confidence in the Lord's plan for goodness in my life.

I grieved the loss alongside my supportive community of believers; strong women of faith who faithfully pointed me back to God and His promises. They reminded me that God works all things for our good according to His purpose; those who love God. A verse I rely on now during trials that test my trust and faith in God's love for me and His promises; Romans 8:28 "And we know that for those who love God all things work together for good, for those who are called according to his purpose."

I was baptized several months after the first procedure to remove the lost pregnancy and during my baptism in the pond at our church I alarmingly found that my body was releasing more of the pregnancy left over! That which was not removed during surgery and was preventing me from being able to conceive again. As shocking and initially embarrassing as that may seem- and it was; I was reminded by those same sisters of faith, that this was a beautiful sign from God. Not to be embarrassed or ashamed of what happened to my body there; that He is in control and loves me and would heal me, and I must trust Him. I began to say to God, *if your will is that I do not give life to a child so be it, and your will be done, and it will go well for me if this is your plan, but if it can be Lord, if it is your will please God let me be able to carry a child in my womb and give birth, bless us with a child, please God.* Some months later we conceived again, and my husband and I have now welcomed into the world our first child, Charlotte Elizabeth Marie. In this case God has answered my prayer, but I saw that I can rest in trusting His timing and relinquishing control to Him. I found peace and joy when I was able to do this. A lesson I had through this was when I compare my life to other's blessings it creates a major obstacle to my own joy and faith walk. It will lead me to not trust in God's good plans for me; so, guarding against comparison is very important for me and us all I believe, and yes, it's easier said than done with all the social media posts and culture norms we live among today- comparison is tempting us all in different forms daily.

FAITH – Many people struggle with having faith when things around them seem to go awry. What would you advise someone who wants to strengthen their faith?

My advice to someone who wants to strengthen their faith is to make a plan of action, such as writing down times you will commit to devoting time with God each day. In committing to embrace patience and compassion for self and others as well as committing to being honest with self and others, what I have experienced is so life-giving when practiced consistently. 1 John 1:9 "If we confess our sins, he is faithful and just to forgive us our sins and to cleanse us from all unrighteousness." Finally, commit to forgiving others no matter who or how deep the offense or pain, even if it is yourself.

I had to learn and accept that forgiveness is not forgetting the pain or hurt. It's not forcing ourselves to trust the one who wronged us but that it is giving the debt to God. Reconciliation is a different step than forgiveness, not to be confused- It's the final step of conflict resolution which happens after both parties take accountability for their own part, ask for forgiveness, and take action steps to earn each other's trust back through healthy boundaries which are important to re-establish trust and relationship.

But forgiveness is giving the offense, pain, hurt; the DEBT against you, to God. Saying, "God, I give this offense to you and I no longer hold this debt over the offender's head." It is the intentional action of telling God, "I trust you for justice and I no longer will seek punishment, retribution, payment or atonement for their sin against me. I will go in peace and hope among the one who hurt me." Colossians 3:13, "Bearing with one another and, if one has a complaint against another, forgiving each other; as the Lord has forgiven you, so you also must forgive."

Give the debt to God, trust him with it, have peace and give peace, even if they don't ask forgiveness for their wrongs or accept their part and try to make things right in all honesty. It's the way to deepen your faith, by first relieving the heavy burden you create for yourself by unforgiveness of self and others.

Follow through on these commitments by finding a trusted friend who knows the Lord. I suggest someone who is a step beyond you in their walk with the Lord to hold you accountable for your commitments and encourage you in truth found in God's word; to point you back to the Lord in love.

Make it a priority to find two or three others of your same sex to be in community with, to admonish, encourage, have accountability with and love and serve alongside; become warriors alongside each other for God.

Two scriptures that help me remember why this community aspect is imperative in my faith walk are; Matthew 18:20 "For Where two or three are gathered in my name, there am I among them." And, James 5:16 "Therefore, confess your sins to one another and pray for one another, that you may be healed. The prayer of a righteous person has great power as it is working."

We are a holy body of believers and God works through us to encourage, admonish, help, serve, strengthen, bless, grow, and sharpen each other and point others to Jesus to be saved by acceptance of Christ's sacrifice on the cross for the forgiveness of sins by God's grace so we can be reconciled to God, have life everlasting with Him and experience His love, power and true life now and forever. We accept the grace we have received by putting our trust in Him and what Christ did for us on the cross. We must trust the importance of being in community with God's people, to do life together as God intended. Don't isolate and deprive yourself and others unintentionally of all that God has in store for you and others through community. Take a leap, reach out, and don't give up--don't ever give up.

OVERCOME - How do you structure your time to reflect all the priorities and opportunities God has given you to be a light for him without losing yourself in the process, both personally and professionally?

To structure my time to reflect all that God has given me to be a light for Him without losing myself I must know when to say *NO;* *o*r as a sweet friend and client of mine would say, *"please hold"* – in her lovely, native British accent. I'm someone who had struggled with boundaries, assertiveness, overextending myself, and stretching myself too thin to people please. When we do this, we are trying to take control rather than allowing God to be in control. When I try to control rather than rely on God with patience, it's led to burn-out, fear of failure, inability to make a move, setbacks, and stagnation in the progress I could have been making had I waited on God or trusted his call on my heart.

I'm inclined to say YES always to people, but to serve others well and honor what God is calling me to do I must have healthy boundaries with others to be honest and say, "I need to pray about this before I commit, and I will get back to you soon, thank you for your patience with me."

If your heart is to do God's work and serve others where you are and are needed, the best thing you can do is allow yourself the space to talk to God and honestly examine your priorities, heart and intentions. What do you think God is calling you to do in this season or that situation. Seek God's will first, found in the Word. If you hastily or over commit yourself to things you set yourself up for failure, and not your best. Saying *no* to something after careful prayer and consideration is serving others well. Honoring God and respecting yourself allows you to say YES to the things God is calling you to do and serve others best.

Being obedient in writing down my values, priorities, obtainable goals and commitments has helped me to weigh other opportunities against these in combination with God's will found in the Word and examine whether it is what God has called me to or not.

I strive to create the space to allow time to pray about how other opportunities will enter my schedule; and fully committing to those which I do accept. Last point; communicating with others is a lost practice in our world today, I believe. To respond in love and patience- responsiveness. Not ignoring others, be it text or email or in person; to take time to RESPOND is loving and needed in our world today. On the other hand, not feeling entitled to getting responses is key as well. Less of me, more of You, God.

OVERCOME - Share with us about a season in your life that God sent you through that changed the course of your life.

For years I struggled with shame, insecurity, and fear of not being accepted by others. My adolescent and early adult years, age 14-29ish could be defined as a young woman running from God and trapped in immense pain; in captivity to the enemy's lies. As I look back now I see how my mother and father where exemplifying the sacrificial and boundless love God has for us all. I refused to trust it. I ran from them and God and took their love for granted. Just like the prodigal son. I was so hurt and angered by life that I couldn't stop running. I desperately wanted to be accepted in a new school at age 14. Being sheltered in a small, safe private school community was what I knew. I was culture shocked and willing to do anything for acceptance. I let myself be used and abused to gain acceptance and I journeyed down a dangerous path for years, trying to be *enough* and accepted. I was giving in to my flesh and comfort idols, feeling further isolated from family; while horribly ashamed and embarrassed the entire time, but I couldn't stop--I hated myself and had little trust in others.

My shame was so deep it took an act of God to break me free from the identity I had placed in my mistakes and failures which had left me feeling judged, judging others, and in a personal prison of the belief I was worthless and no good, capable of only calamity and pain. But God never gave up on me. He chased me down and finally He had me, once and for all. After accepting and believing what Jesus did for me on the cross, that He died for all my past, present and future sins, that I was forgiven for eternity and wiped clean as snow by God's grace; I surrendered my life over to God. That's when it was like the chains from hell over my life had been broken and I was literally set free.

Since then, my ability to *receive* God's love for me, trust His TRUE LOVE for me, has worked to anchor me firmly in his hands. More and more this LOVE is pouring out to love others and I'm able to forgive easier, surrender more freely to Him, like when I am tempted or find myself in the storms of life. Blessings abound in my life today and I am so thankful and grateful to just be alive today and know the love of God. I desire this more than money, a fancy car, big house, fame, beauty, worldly success or any other worldly desire. I am satisfied and thankful for what I do have and in Christ.

I know that I am a broken sinner saved by God's amazing grace, not by my own good deeds-- I'm in constant need of a savior, and I'm reminded of how I fall short of God's standard daily, but I strive to be godly despite my nature. I don' t identify with the girl I once was. However, I have compassion and understanding for that young woman, and I forgive her. I have had to grieve her and all she went through. I have a new life, transforming and new in Christ. God's boundless and sacrificial love never gives up on us no matter how far we've strayed or how broken we are. Love really does conquer all. I am fully aware of the nightmare of my flesh that awaits me if I am to become untethered to God, but now I have hope and faith in God's power in me to overcome all things, and I work to remain in Him through Christ by His grace. I'm an imperfect sinner, in need of a savior.

POUR -What three scriptures would you share with someone if they are in a season of transition and need clarity? Also, share why you selected these three scriptures.

Three scriptures for when you find yourself in a season of transition needing clarity; there are so many but here's three; 1) Proverbs 15:22 "Without counsel plans fail, but with many advisers they succeed."

I selected this scripture because our common flesh nature is to seek to control things and to arrogantly go our own way, seeking our personal comforts and thinking ourselves better and wiser than we really are. That is why guidance and counsel of many others; God's people, our community of believers are imperative to us. It is wise to create that space for counsel and careful consideration rather than acting hastily, which can trip us up to falling victim to Satan's temptation traps and lies.

2) Philippian 4:6-7 "Do not be anxious about anything, but in everything by prayer and supplication with thanksgiving let your requests be made known to God. And the peace of God, which

surpasses all understanding, will guard your hearts and your minds in Christ Jesus."

I must rely on prayer to give me peace. It leads me to lean on God and trust Him with everything. If you don't know what to pray for, that's okay, just pray. God already knows what you need and what you're asking via the Holy Spirit. Just start by giving thanks for things you are grateful and ask Him to guide your steps and open your eyes to His will. - Remember He only wants what is good for you, His beloved child, no matter how bleak or untrue this may seem now.

3.) <u>Proverbs 3:5-6</u> "Trust in the Lord with all you heart, and do not lean on your own understanding. In all your ways acknowledge Him and He will make straight your paths."

This is probably one of my favorite scriptures that I've committed to memory. While in the marriage community of Re-Engage with my husband at our church, the wife of the leader couple had all the ladies in our group commit this one to memory, and I am so thankful. It has and will continue to guide my steps. It helps keep me stay or return back on course through life's winding paths. Not my own understanding do I need, but to trust in you, Lord; make my paths straight to life everlasting.

POUR -What is your favorite scripture, and how has that influenced your role as a woman who works and walks by faith?

My favorite scripture up to this point and will always be my top I believe, is 1Peter 5:10, "And after you have suffered a little while, the God of all grace, who has called you to His eternal glory in

Christ, will Himself restore, confirm, strengthen, and establish you. To Him be the dominion forever and ever."

What this scripture means to me, is that it serves as a strong reminder to first and foremost put God on the throne of my heart-above all others and all other things. Daily, and as often as needed, checking that God is the ruler of my life and heart; my only King and Master. It can be a real struggle to humble myself to do this; to be honest about what or who may be taking God's place on the throne, sometimes myself.

Secondly, this scripture is such a SWEET promise God gave us through his divinely inspired Word found in the gospel here! It speaks everything to me coming from the shame, pain, fear, and doom I once was imprisoned by. It tells me that I can rest in peace at night and when God calls me home at the end of my life, knowing that what God has started in me in this life will be completed. I can be released from comparison, envy, and despair for lack of worldly things; because what God has in store for us in eternity is more than any human desire could fathom to be desired; that level of joy peace and love- imagine. In this I rest my hope and in exchange have lasting joy, strength and hope.

And finally, it tells me that when I pick up the cross to follow Christ and die to my flesh as Jesus literally did for us, I will experience His promises in my life now; which I experience more and more the stronger I become in my faith walk, relinquishing control to God. I am restored, confirmed, strengthened, and established in Christ by God's grace and power.

My hope and belief are that the work God started in me in this life will be completed when I go to eternal life with Him and the body of believers after this life is over. The best is yet to come. This is our opportunity to experience the gift of life in Christ Jesus now in this life and prepare and build for eternity with our Father in heaven in the next. I don't want anyone to miss out on all God has for them in this life or the next, but more than I could ever want for others, God desires this for all mankind, that no one shall perish, who accept his perfect sacrifice in Jesus's death on a cross and resurrection, because He loves us ALL more than we can humanly comprehend. Don't miss out in all that God has for you. It's never too late to surrender and receive salvation while you still have breath in your lungs.

Any closing thoughts?

Let us always remember God's great commandment given to us by Jesus, John 13:34 "A new commandment I give to you, that you love one another: just as I have loved you, you also are to love one another." Let go of people pleasing, comparison, showing off, judging others, rudeness in disguise of 'directness', self-righteousness, and being wise in our own eyes.

Let us be mindful not to be wise in our own eyes, remaining humble and in humility thinking more of others than ourselves; not in an insecure type of way but in a selfless way, as in Jesus's examples; less of me more of you; God, and more of you; (other person)--Philippians 2:3 "Do nothing from selfish ambition or conceit, but in humility count others more significant than yourselves."

Let us remain open to being vulnerable with others and to practice vulnerability and honesty with those who have earned trust in our life; to practice honesty and forgiveness, consistently. To commit to being compassionate to ourselves and others through patience, grace, understanding, and hope. And finally, to give thanks and practice gratitude, which has broken me through the worst sadness or depressions I've ever faced.

Dear Reader, you are so infinitely loved by our Father. more than we can humanly ever conceive. And though God is in heaven, He is right here next to you, now. I pray you grow in your faith walk, that you grow to deepen your relationship with God, that you let God in and experience His love for you as it overflows into others and you point them to the cross and to the only one who can truly heal them and make them whole in this life. I pray you trust the life God has in store for you when you fully surrender and put your trust in Christ's sacrifice and God's love and provision for you.

Friend, be patient with yourself, be kind to yourself, and have compassion and grace for yourself. Forgive yourself. Love yourself. Remember others; they are imperfect like you. Give them grace like God gave you. As Christians, we are imperfect humans, but we serve a perfect God so trust in Him for all things in your life. May God bless you and keep you.

If you haven't surrendered to God and accepted and believed in the salvation and reconciliation He provided to you fulfilled through Jesus on the cross and His resurrection, or if you have turned from your faith or are far from God, I pray you trust our Father, God will never give up calling you to come home to Him, to your true family. Jesus Christ will take you home- follow. Remember God's power in weakness--Come as you are today.

INDIA
WHITE

Tell us a little about yourself.

Hi, my name is India White, and I am an author, motivational speaker and educator. I have been serving as a math teacher, assistant principal and math coach for the past 10 years in Florida public schools. Through the years, I've shared my story of overcoming homelessness my last two years of high school to help raise funds for students across the state. As a result, working with organizations like Take Stock in Children, YMCA, Hillsborough Education Foundation and others, we've seen MILLIONS of dollars raised in scholarships for scholars across the state!

This success has birthed a new chapter of embracing the author in my as I've been blessed to write a book series on "Overcoming Obstacles" as well as a book on Success titled, "Success in a Book." I have been able to work with various women and students at book signings, conferences, workshops, and churches to help empower them and help people to overcoming every obstacle and thrive in their calling! Through various book signings in Tampa, Sarasota and more, I've been privileged to learn from other leaders and connect with those who are doing the same to serve their community.

My purpose is to inspire others through sharing my story as an author and motivational speaker. I am also called to pay it forward by working as an educator with other educational leaders.

The chapter I cherish about my life the most is the chapter of motherhood. I have an amazing daughter and son who have been part of the reason why I continue to pursue success. I enjoy trips on the beach with my family and feel very connected to them. We enjoy attending church together, where I love to go and worship God and serve in the ministry.

Share with us what your business/ministry is and what it does for those that you serve.

I am grateful to say that I have just began my business, "Rising Glory Productions". Our mission is to provide services that will uplift, inspire and empower others through speaking, conferences and other resources.

Rising Glory Productions is the avenue in which I can see my book series "How to Overcome Obstacles from Your Past" to various customers, as well as hold book signings, workshops, conferences, coaching sessions and more!

I do my best to give my all as a minister of Christ in the fullest capacity. Working with other business owners, churches and leaders has established a sense of hope in the community that the best is yet to come. I love what I do, and I know I am called to serve and learn from others as I continue to write books, speak and work with others to provide desired and needed resources to the community.

DIRECTION - Sometimes people are confused in recognizing and knowing what they are called to do by the Lord. What advice would you share in how one can hear and know what God has called them to do?

When someone is trying to know what their calling is from the Lord, it is imperative that they first learn how to hear God's voice. Sometimes God will speak clearly through a dream or vision; other times he will speak via Ramah word. This requires sincere and keen seeking of God's voice in quiet time (40+ min) alone with God as well as praying and opening one's spirit to find the direction of God.

I can remember consecrating myself for a time and as I worshipped God about my career, he told me, "I want you to teach." It was then that I realized that my purpose would be fulfilled in the realm of education. However, God has continued to speak since then and the calling has continued to evolve. Whenever God has a desire to share his purpose with an individual, he knows exactly how to go about doing it. He is Big and Bad and God enough to do anything he sets his mind to…remember that. Sometimes, God will use a proven prophet or prophetess to also confirm what he is saying directly to someone about their purpose. Remember, God is love, and he wants the best for his children. The word of God says that he will withhold no good thing to them that love him. So, be encouraged and practice principles that will help you hear the Lord for YOURSELF!

DIRECTION – There are times when someone may struggle with really knowing their gifts and how to use them. How did you know what you were gifted in, and how do you apply that in your life?

I believe that the gifts and the calling of God are without repentance. What I've found is that people will have "spooky" moments in which they will be able to tell someone a word of wisdom or have a prophetic utterance or even see things in the spirit that will come true. It's in times like these that a born-again believer must discipline themselves and chase God to find out exactly what their gifts are and how they should be operating in them. This takes effort, respect for the gifts and time. The Bible says to "let everything be done decently and in order." Therefore, everyone who desires to operate in their gifts, mentioned in 1st Corn. 14, must take time to seek God for THEIR gifts and the purpose behind having the gift. Then, during their time at church, during work or whenever

God finds it appropriate, they should utilize the gift and step out in faith as a person who flows in the gifts.

For example, I think of Samuel the prophet in the Old Testament, who whenever he was 6 years old began to hear from the Lord. As he grew older, he consecrated himself and made himself available to God. As a result, he served as a tried and true prophet for many leaders including Saul. This took years of building and discipline on Samuel's part, and God walked him through the process. I believe that God is not a respecter of persons and will do the same for anyone that is HUNGRY to know what their gifts are and how to properly flow in them. The Lord will train his people.

DIRECTION - Many people struggle with developing a habit of including God in all that they do. How do you make God a part of your life/business/ministry each day?

Proverbs 3:5-6 says to trust in the Lord with all your heart and lean not unto thine own understanding; in all thy ways acknowledge him and he will direct your paths.

If people live with this verse written on their hearts, they won't be able to go without acknowledging the Lord. Sometimes, whenever an individual is trying to kindle their fire for God and have a zeal and passion that helps them keep God first, they must begin to make habits of meditating on the word of God like Psalms 50 exemplifies. They must CHOOSE to think on God and his goodness and to meditate on verses, Godly songs, and seek the voice of God throughout the day. The Bible also mentions that we should pray without ceasing. This is another way people can make sure that God is a part of everything they do.

Furthermore, whenever they desire to include God in their ministry, business etc., all they must do is welcome him in and acknowledge him. God is omnipresent, meaning he is everywhere. Therefore, they can't keep anything secret, so they might as well bring God along! God is exciting about our future and hopes to give everyone an expected end (Jeremiah 29:11), so people must believe this and embrace God in every area of their lives, so they can give him Glory and enjoy his blessings.

FAITH - As a woman of faith, what has been your biggest obstacle or challenge in your faith walk with God, and how did you navigate that successfully?

The biggest challenge of my faith has been to know that God can and that he will, but to wait on his TIMING for the promise or miracle to come to pass. MANY times, in my life, Jesus has been an on-time God…literally! Sometimes, I'm an inch away from unbelief or being tempted to curse God and die, but God pulls through right at the spur of the moment. This is true faith being tested, but I know that his mercy helps me prevail in the end, and he gets ALL the glory once it's all said and done.

Also, I find that sometimes God will trust you to carry personal "crosses". In times like these, you must learn to trust God's big picture over your temporary one. Learning to say, "Not my will but thine be done" is the hardest thing sometimes to say. However, when you are truly IN LOVE WITH JESUS, you will learn to adjust your heart's desires with his. Nothing will move you and you won't be offended in Him.

FAITH – Many people struggle with having faith when things around them seem to go awry. What would you advise someone who wants to strengthen their faith?

I think it's exciting when people are seeking to strengthen their faith. However, they must remember that Hebrews 11 says that "faith is the substance of things hoped for, the evidence of things not seen." Also, they must remember that "death and life are in the power of the tongue… (Prov. 18:21)." With these scriptures, they must have enough faith to speak their desires into existence and to thank and praise God in advance like they already have what they are believing for.

People who are really trying to increase their faith must also remember the power in "touching and agreeing". Scripture says that where "two or three or gathered, there will I be in the midst of them." Therefore, sometimes joining with others for agreement will help strengthen faith and get prayers answered. Stretching faith is a great process.

In addition, it is pleasing to God whenever an individual is increasing their faith. The bible talks about the first people on the list to hell are the fearful and the unbelieving. This is not the time to DOUBT but to believe God even more that he is able to do exceeding abundantly above all that we can ask or think. Therefore, a person who is truly trying to please God must get honest and open with the Lord and express to God, "I believe, but Lord, help thou mine unbelief." Then, they need to step back and WATCH GOD! Amen!!

OVERCOME - How do you structure your time to reflect all the priorities and opportunities God has given you to be a light for him without losing yourself in the process, both personally and professionally?

Sometimes, you have to learn how to say NO. I find that people will want me to do a, b, and c, and sometimes, I can only meet the expectations of a and b. Therefore, I have to be firm in my decision and decide when to say yes and when to say no. The priority is usually God, family and then my career. If anything is extra, then I eliminate it. I once heard from an expert in time management that we are to make time for things that are most valuable first, then fit in the "little" stuff. Yes, this is easier said than done, but once someone begins creating a habit of this practice, life will flow smoother.

In addition, I remember to do all for the Glory of God. I do all in the name of the Lord Jesus Christ. Hence, this brings with it a sense of responsibility and accountability. I make sure to hold myself accountable with leaders and to God. In addition, I consider future generation and my children who might look up to me and constantly consider the example I'd like to set for them. I am not an island unto myself; hence, I always perform at my best. Plus, it's always exciting to see the outcome when you give it your all!

OVERCOME - Share with us about a season in your life that God sent you through that changed the course of your life.

I went through a season of transition as soon as I moved to Tampa, Fl. While in Tampa, I was an educator that became teacher of the Year and was shortly promoted to Assistant Principal for 3 years. This was a "high" time in my life and I loved being a leader with much responsibility working with other leaders. However, in my personal life, I went through much grief. The same year I obtained my Master's degree in Ed. Leadership, I lost my sister to Breast cancer. The same year I was promoted to Asst. Principal, I lost my father. Then, the following year, as a doctoral student, I lost my mother to Pancreatic Cancer. I had to be there very closely to prepare arrangements while remaining strong for my family members. In this season, I was shaken to the core of me. I began to say, "Whatever God" because I grew numb inside. I believed God to heal every one of them. His sovereignty stepped in and he decided to take them. I was crushed and confused. I had fasted, prayed, believed God, had prayer chains going, was in repentant mode etc. However, I felt like God let me down.

During this time, the Lord spoke to me, and let me know that I was still his Bride. I was scared, nervous, confused, depressed, and angry and felt all alone. However, my walk with God became deeper and more intimate than ever before. I learned that life does go on after much grief and that you can smile again once the test is finished. So, I carried my cross of grief while praising God despite it all. As a result, my nieces (deceased sister's children) were born again at a Pentecostal church. They both graduated from college. We've picked up the pieces together and celebrate the rest of the joy that has remained after. We choose to cherish the memories of these great people of our heritage while pleasing God and representing them well with every accomplishment we make moving forward.

POUR -What three scriptures would you share with someone if they are in a season of transition and need clarity? Also, share why you selected these three scriptures.

1) **Psalm 118:17- "I shall not die, but live and declare the works of the Lord." –**

This is my "go to" verse anytime I am in the valley of life. I always encourage myself by saying, "You're not gonna die in this!" This is important because sometimes life will make it seem like you will die.

Since the enemy is constantly trying to convince Saints that they will fall short and that God doesn't love them, it is imperative to have a verse that reminds them of the opposite. This verse lets an individual know that they will eventually come out strong on the other side and declare the works of the Lord.

When an individual is in transition, sometimes the road can become foggy and they don't have an incline as to what they are supposed to do or how the outcome of a situation will turn out. This is when they need to take a step back, wait on God and declare that they won't die, but live and declare the works of the Lord.

2) **Micah 3:7-8-Rejoice not against me, O my enemy: when I fall, I shall arise; when I sit in darkness, the LORD shall be a light unto me.**

In this Christian walk, there will be MANY hang-ups and personal disappointments. In addition, we will fail others who rely on us. In times like these, we must remind the enemy and those who are for our down fall to rejoice not against us and that when we fall we shall arise. Failure is not the end of the chapter for us! We are unbeatable because of Jesus who lives inside of us!

Sometimes, people can become discouraged as they see people pointing the finger at them and saying "Aha, aha, our eye hath seen it.", or will mock their belief in God because things went awry from the expected. It's in times like these that they need to remind their enemies that when they fall, they SHALL arise, and when they are in DARKNESS, the Lord will be a light unto them. This verse really "completes the big picture" for every believer, and gives them something to rise for and to hope in.

3) "Job 23:10- But he knoweth the way that I take: *when he hath tried me, I shall come forth as gold.*"

It is imperative that a believer or a Christian understands that there will be mountain tops and valleys in their walk with God. Therefore, they must trust God with the process and know that when he is finished trying them, they will come forth as gold. This will help them stay the course and not faint before the promise arises.

In addition, knowing that the hardships an individual brings growth, strength and depth to a believer's walk with God helps that person to embrace a mindset in which they can endure hardness as a good soldier. This takes away the thoughts that everything must be a bed of roses in life. This will not always be the case.

Furthermore, when an individual knows that God knows the way that they take, they won't be so worried about making the right choice all by themselves; they will trust in God's leading and will wait on the Lord to iron out the way for them.

POUR -What is your favorite scripture, and how has that influenced your role as a woman who works and walks by faith?

<u>**Favorite Scripture:**</u> **Psalm 118: 17- "I shall not die, but live, and declare the works of the Lord."**

As a new born-again believer, and a believer that has done my best to strive in excellence as a Christian, this verse has been there with me as I grieved the death of my sister, brother, mother and father, and while suffering through various hardships in life. When I think of this verse, I think of how it's almost a prophetic declaration to oneself that they will not die but live and…. they are declaring that they will not die in a dilemma nor be defeated.

I love to think of how as I've been able to walk by faith and grow in faith how this verse has carried me from "glory to glory" and has inspired me to move forward despite disappointment and the unexpected. This verse has served as an ultimate encouragement because it forces everyone to "look up" and to place hope in their tomorrow. I believe that the defeat of a believer begins when they stop hoping in God and in their future and their purpose and believe the lies of the enemy. This can be avoided as they meditate on this scripture. Then, once they begin to see their life turn around, they can increase their faith and give the glory to God for working everything out and seeing them through the process.

Any closing thoughts?

1. Never settle, fight the urge to be average, pursue your destiny and remember that promotion comes to you!

2. In addition, never fight against flesh and blood. Let the Lord fight for you and watch him work everything out on your behalf.

3. Furthermore, trusting in God is a process and it takes an act of the will of man. Trusting God will never feel easy but knowing that he is just, and his sovereignty is fair is something that can cause everyone to know that the Lord won't fail them.

4. Also, when all else fails, choose to BELIEVE God and stand on HIS truth presented in the Word of God.

5. Know God; he's coming back for a people that KNOW HIM and worship him in Spirit and in Truth (John 4).

6. Try God; Become a born-again believer (Acts 2:38, John 3:5) and allow him to mold your life

7. Seek God regularly for direction; trust his leading

8. Embrace accountability

9. Remember, life is not a bed of roses but more like a battleship. Don't burn out or get offended along the process

10. Find a reason to smile every day; life is too short to be miserable.

KELSI MATA

Tell us a little about yourself.

I am not one of those people who grew up in the church and became a Christian at an early age. My family was great, but we were not the church goers that we are now. As a family we would attend church occasionally, maybe four times a year. It was a very rare occurrence in our household. We were more on the CEO side of the spectrum (Christmas/Easter only). I was not oblivious to the name "Jesus", but I never had an actual relationship with Him either. Occasionally, I would be sent to church camps with my friends and hear His name, but I personally was there for the social aspect.

Around the age of eleven, my household took a dramatic turn. My parents were getting divorced. When the divorce happened, this caused a lot of confusion on commitment and trust. When you see the two most important people in your life go their separate ways it raises questions. Throughout the years I was traveling back and forth from my mom's house to my dad's house. When I was 18, I started dating a guy who I felt I would spend my life with. We dated for 3 ½ years on and off. It was a very unhealthy relationship full of abuse, lies, and sexual sin. We lived together outside of wedlock. I had no clue what the true meaning of love was and wrestled with low self-worth.

When I was 19, I got a call from my dad that would change the course of my life forever. My dad had been diagnosed with stage 4 pancreatic cancer. He passed away a year later. This left me with hatred and anger towards God. My depression and suicidal thoughts were at an all-time high. The passing of my father and a breakup that crushed me. Eventually this led me down a destructive path. I found myself partying and engaging with the wrong crowd. My nights consisted of drinking, smoking weed and searching for affection from others. Even though I was doing all these things I still had a void that could not be filled. One day as I was scrolling through Instagram, I came across a photo one of my friends posted. It was picture of a cross with sins nailed to it. Sins like adultery, porn, anxiety, and pride. There was a red line marked through all of them. I reached out and asked him where this was taken, and he said The Porch at Watermark. Not too long after that I went to the Porch to check it out. What I thought would be a one-time thing turned into an every Tuesday occurrence. After attending for a few months, I learned the truth about the undeniable love of God. I finally began to understand the good news of Jesus. I realized that I was a slave to my own desires and needed a great savior. God sent His son Jesus to die and pay the price of my debts. This sacrifice was a true representation of His love and grace. He was buried with our transgressions and God raised Him from the dead proving that He could defeat all sin. 2 Corinthians 5:17-18, *"Therefore, if anyone is in Christ, he is a new creation. The old has passed away; behold, the new has come."* All this is from God, who through Christ reconciled us to himself and gave us the ministry of reconciliation.

Even after I found Christ it was not easy. Following the time after I accepted Christ, I went through a break up that led me through a dark time. This time I was at a point where I wanted to take my own life. It was my old self coming back to haunt me. But by the grace of God, He rescued me from my selfish desires. During this season life began to change. I began Regeneration through Watermark Community Church which is a 12-step ministry for people who feel their life is broken. Through community and reading the word of God, my heart began to seek to know Him and the true gift of forgiveness. I knew my life before Christ was meaningless and because of Him I have a new life and I have been set free.

Share with us what your business/ministry is and what it does for those that you serve.

The ministries that I am involved in now are The Porch and Christfit. The Porch is a young adult's ministry for 20 and 30-year olds. The mission statement at the Porch is "Surrendered to God, we are changing the world through the lives of young adults." The hope is that this ministry would reach the lives of young adults and continue to spread the love of Christ. The Porch is a place where 3,000 young adults gather on Tuesday nights to hear the goodness of our Lord. Our hope is to help young adults understand what it means to follow Christ in today's culture.

There are different teams that you can serve on at the Porch. I am on a team called Welcome Mat. Our team role is to welcome new Porch-goers, a.k.a Porchies with intentionality and the goal of guiding conversations toward Jesus Christ. We educate new comers on various ministries that The Porch and Watermark have to offer while also answering challenging questions. We follow up and connect with those who are new to The Porch. The Porch is a large gathering and can be a little overwhelming for someone who is new. That is why we want to make sure all feel welcomed and loved.

The other ministry I volunteer at is Christfit. Christfit Unashamed is a place to build each other up, serve one another and connect to the body through the Crossfit methods. Christfit is on Sundays at 3pm. At Christfit you can expect community, a great workout, and time in the word. We start out our time with a warm up and then meet and greet time. This allows newcomers to meet the Christfit crew. Following this we do a Crossfit workout, typically this is a partner workout. Once the workout is completed, we then circle up for devotional time. Different volunteers each week will share a devotional or what they have been learning from the Lord. It is a unique environment to come together as a community and have fellowship. It's all about faith, fellowship and fitness! As a volunteer, I help assist people with sign in and demonstrating movements. We reach out when people request more information or seek pastoral care. We pray for the ministry and that it glorifies the Lord in all that it does.

DIRECTION - Sometimes people are confused in recognizing and knowing what they are called to do by the Lord. What advice would you share in how one can hear and know what God has called them to do?

Scripture shows that we are called to be disciples and live on mission in all walks of life. As Acts 20:24 states "But I do not account my life of any value nor as precious to myself, if only I may finish my course and the ministry that I received from the Lord Jesus, to testify to the gospel of the grace of God." Our calling as Christians is to carry out the mission anywhere we are and share the good news which is the gospel. Many people put so much emphasis on what the Lord is calling them to do when all the Lord asks is that we make disciples of the nations. He teaches us to obey all His commands. Matthew 28:18-20 "And Jesus came and said to them, "All authority in heaven and on earth has been given to me. Go therefore and make disciples of all nations, baptizing them in the name of the Father and of the Son and of the Holy Spirit, teaching them to observe all that I have commanded you. And behold, I am with you always, to the end of the age." Now I know, this can be intimidating or scary to some because there is a fear of what will someone think of you if you bring up Jesus. The truth is, it is the most important conversation to have. You have those conversations because you truly care and love those people. If I ignore this calling and never share the gift of God, it is the most hurtful thing I could do. God has placed you right where you need to be at the exact right moment.

DIRECTION – There are times when someone may struggle with really knowing their gifts and how to use them. How did you know what you were gifted in, and how do you apply that in your life?

I honestly feel like I am not sure what I am gifted in or where I'm supposed to be. All I know is that whenever I serve, it brings out what the Lord is teaching me and how the Lord is wanting me to grow. Serving others takes humility. Philippians 2:2-3 "Do nothing from selfish ambition or conceit, but in humility count others more significant than yourselves. Let each of you look not only to his own interests, but also to the interests of others." If I have to serve others, am I going to be upset when I do or am I going to love them more than I love myself? I feel like applying that to my everyday life. It is important but is not easy. It takes breaking down barriers and walls. How do others perceive the way that I am treating them? Am I thinking about them before myself? And throughout all this, am I relying on the Lord throughout it all. I listen and take it to heart where the Lord is calling me.1 Peter 4:10-11, "As each has received a gift, use it to serve one another, as good stewards of God's varied grace: whoever speaks, as one who speaks oracles of God; whoever serves, as one who serves by the strength that God supplies—in order that in everything God may be glorified through Jesus Christ. To him belong glory and dominion forever and ever. Amen."

DIRECTION - Many people struggle with developing a habit of including God in all that they do. How do you make God a part of your life/business/ministry each day?

Prayer is crucial to my walk with the Lord. I must constantly pray throughout my day. He gives me the guidance I need. I must continuously hand my anxiety over to Him. At work I take the time to pray. Not later but right then and there. How do people see me at work? Can they tell that I am a Christian or do they question whether I am or not? I do have intentional conversations with people at my work. With where I work right now, I have a great opportunity and platform to do that because I meet so many people every day. The ministry that I serve in has taught me how to have conversations and include the Lord in my everyday life. I strive to be a light to others and pray people see that. This helps me to have a closer relationship with God because I know the importance of devoting, praying and relying on Him daily. I constantly remind myself that He has redeemed me from the pit I was in and saved me. I need to be gracious towards that. Just take the time to be quiet with Him and allowing my heart to be open to whatever He has planned for me that day. Colossians 1:9-10 "And so, from the day we heard, we have not ceased to pray for you, asking that you may be filled with the knowledge of his will in all spiritual wisdom and understanding, so as to walk in a manner worthy of the Lord, fully pleasing to him: bearing fruit in every good work and increasing in the knowledge of God."

FAITH - As a woman of faith, what has been your biggest obstacle or challenge in your faith walk with God, and how did you navigate that successfully?

If I am being completely authentic, when I first began my faith walk, I did not it navigate successfully. Instead I had a complete breakdown. As a recent follower of Christ, I think I was naive in my thinking process. I thought that maybe life would get better or easier now that Jesus was in the picture but that was not the case. Not too long after accepting Christ, I went through a difficult breakup that left me feeling unworthy, unloved, and alone. It had been a buildup of many things in my life that eventually pushed me to unthinkable circumstances.

Instead of trusting that the Lord had this under control, I wanted to escape the pain that my broken heart was feeling. My past began to creep in and my suicidal thoughts began to fill my head. I was a complete mess. My life had been so focused on what this world had to offer and not God. These thoughts got bad to the point where I contemplated how I could leave this world and not have any more pain. I had written my letter and was waiting for the time to make it happen. Don't worry; I am getting to the part where my faith walk begins to navigate successfully. My mom had been so worried one night that she was dialing the number to the hospital. It was there I realized I did need help.

During this season, I began a ministry called Regeneration. This was a 12-step ministry for people who feel their life is broken. I think of 1 Corinthians 10:13 "No temptation has overtaken you that is not common to man. God is faithful, and he will not let you be tempted beyond your ability, but with the temptation he will always provide the way of escape, that you may be able to endure it." At the time I may have felt that my world was crashing. I had this mindset that all these important men in my life continued to either leave or be taken from me. I felt the depression and suicidal thoughts began after my father passed and I buried those deep down by living for the world. Once this breakup happened though I felt the reoccurring feeling but the Lord finally did a breakthrough with my hardened heart. Once in Regeneration, my focus was on my relationship with the Lord and the struggles that I faced. God revealed himself more and more and was slowly providing this escape from my past. This temporary heartache would heal and with God as my stronghold I knew that my faith would prevail.

FAITH – Many people struggle with having faith when things around them seem to go awry. What would you advise someone who wants to strengthen their faith?

James 1:2-3 "Count it all joy, my brothers, when you meet trail of various kinds, for you know that the testing of your faith produces steadfastness." Strengthening your faith takes dedication and devotion. In life we are going to have our fair share of trails and struggles. These struggles can either knock you down completely or have you running after the Lord harder. When we are taken off guard and we feel like are faith is being shaken, we must trust that God is in control. Through these tests we can get stronger, bolder, and persistent in our faith. Let me put it this way, what exactly do we need to stay physically healthy? There is food and exercise. If we do not eat we will grow weak and if we do not exercise may not be as helpful to others. This can also be said for our spiritual growth. God has given us the spiritual food needed for use to become stronger in our faith. He did this by giving us His word (the Bible), prayer, and community with other believers. If it was not for these three things my faith could not grow. I surround myself with other brothers and sisters in Christ. Hebrews 10:24-25 "Let us consider how we may spur one another on toward love and good deeds, not giving up meeting together." Honestly, this has helped me so much when I have others surrounding me who love Jesus!

OVERCOME - How do you structure your time to reflect all the priorities and opportunities God has given you to be a light for him without losing yourself in the process, both personally and professionally?

I am learning to be better with my time and how I fill it. I used to be the biggest people pleaser and hated to turn down opportunities. Throughout the years though, I have found that sometimes too much of a good thing can also leave you lost. Personally, I must be aware of how I am spending my time. Is this beneficial for my walk? Will this take away from my time with the Lord? Am I doing this for Him or myself? Professionally, I keep in mind that as a Christian I am called to a higher standard. I want to be as much as representation of Christ as I can. 1 Corinthians 10:31 "So, whether you eat or drink, or whatever you do, do all to the glory of God." The Lord says in *whatever* we do we need to *glorify* Him and that does not mean the workplace is any different.

Dependence is a huge thing both personally and professionally. I go to work utterly dependent on the Lord because without Him I can't breathe, talk, or even move. I cannot be of any spiritual influence to others if I do not have that dependency on Him. John 15:5 "I am the vine; you are the branches. Whoever abides in me and I in him, he it is that bears much fruit, for apart from me you can do nothing." That is exactly what I strive to do. Always abide in Him daily because without Him I can do nothing. I think that is why I love that verse so much. The visual I see is beautiful. The branches must always be attached to the vine or else they will die, and no fruit can come from them. So daily we must keep our dependence on Him to not lose sight of our purpose.

OVERCOME - Share with us about a season in your life that God sent you through that changed the course of your life.

In 2011 my life went from normal to being completely destructive. The reason I start with this is because it leads up to where I am now. The Lord took me through one extremely difficult season that sent me running. I would like to say running for the Lord but in fact it was the complete opposite. August of 2011 is the year that my dad passed away from his battle with pancreatic cancer. I'd love to sit here and say that during this time I found the Lord and trusted in His goodness, but I didn't. I had no intentions of giving any glory to this so called "God". I remember that night going outside and crying in tears that I hated God and if He was so good why would something like this happen.

As I mentioned earlier, this led me down a path that was unhealthy in many aspects. I devalued myself by having inappropriate relations with men. I drank consistently and smoked weed on a regular basis. I was living life for myself and honestly could care less what happened to me at that time. This season went on for many years and didn't stop until I decided to check out the Porch in 2015. Now this wasn't just a coincidence, the Lord had a plan with it all. The whole reason I knew about the Porch was because a friend from college posted a picture from the Porch it.

During these Tuesday nights I began to hear truth and everything that was said felt as though it was directed towards me. It began to set a fire in my heart. I was not promised that my life would be easy, and it wasn't. In John 16:33 it says "I have said these things to you, that in me you may have peace. In the world you will have tribulation. But take heart; I have overcome the world." This truth applied then, now and will continue to for the rest of my life. Ezekiel

36:26 "And I will give you a new heart, and a new spirit I will put within you. And I will remove the heart of stone from your flesh and give you a heart of flesh." This is exactly what the Lord was doing. He was stirring my affections and taking my harden heart and making it His. He was opening my eyes to so much more than I could have imagined. The loss of my father was hard, but I know that the Lord has a purpose for everything that we face in life. It may have taken me several years in a season of doubt, hurt, and brokenness but God prevailed and broke through that bondage.

POUR -What three scriptures would you share with someone if they are in a season of transition and need clarity? Also, share why you selected these three scriptures.

John 10:10 "The thief comes only to steal and kill and destroy. I came that they may have life and have it abundantly." This verse is a favorite of mine. When I am going through change and feel as though I am being attacked, this verse speaks to me. There is an enemy looking to destroy all that we are, and our only hope is Jesus. God sent His Son so that we would have life and live it fully for Him. We have salvation and hope in the name of Jesus. Even though this world may try to cut you down, know that we always have life and a comforter with us. He brings us eternal life!

2 Corinthians 3:17" Now the Lord is the Spirit, and where the Spirit of the Lord is, there is freedom. "I chose this one because I tend to down play the Holy Spirit. The Lord sent the Holy Spirit as a *helper*. (John 16:7) It shows that the spirit is always with us and we have freedom in that. We are not bound by our sins anymore! Another reason I love this one, is because there is a song by Shane and Shane called "Liberty". It's one of my all-time favorites. It references this verse. It signifies victory and that because of what

Jesus did we are free. We are never alone because once we believe in Him; the Holy Spirit is forever with us.

Isaiah 41:10 "Fear not, for I am with you; be not dismayed, for I am your God; I will strengthen you, I will help you, I will uphold you with my righteous right hand." This verse says so much. Fear is something we all face. God is with us through all walks of life. He is the strength we need to get through each season. We must take this truth to heart even when things do not seem clear. He makes many profound statements. I am your *God*, I will *strengthen* you, and I will *help* you. God will uphold me through it all.

POUR -What is your favorite scripture, and how has that influenced your role as a woman who works and walks by faith?

Oh, my favorite scripture. That is a hard one because I feel like I could talk about so many! I feel the one that has influenced me a lot lately, especially being a 27-year-old single woman is 1 Samuel 16:7. "But the Lord said to Samuel, "Do not look on his appearance of on the height of his stature, because I have rejected him. For the Lord sees not as man sees: man looks on the outward appearance, but the Lord looks on the heart." Our society is obsessed about outward appearances and how others perceive us. I am guilty of feeling insecure, unworthy, or that I do not measure up to the standards of today's generation. None of that matters though. What is truly important is what is in our hearts and that our affections are for the Lord. As God's daughter you are loved, adored and cared for. He sees you and knows everything about you. I know I tend to forget that often, but the Lord constantly reminds me that I am His! I keep this quote at my desk at work "As the daughter of the King your purpose is not to turn heads, your purpose is to turn hearts toward the King." The Lord wants are hearts to be stirred and devoted to

Him. He is the one who gives us purpose. We are to glorify Him in all that we do. Do not let this world make you think less of yourself because I know I have been down that road and it is a dead end. Allow the Lord to change your heart and desires to what matters most, His saving grace!

Any closing thoughts?

Walk boldly in your faith knowing that He is there through the storm. That He saves, redeems, and restores all who are broken. He is a provider, comforter, helper and healer. The Lord is good, He is so good. We all need a savior and Jesus Christ is the answer. He offers this gift of salvation. Take it, share it, and glorify it! All for His kingdom!

LATON
CANGELOSE

Tell us a little about yourself.

I love the Lord Jesus Christ with all my heart! I was born and raised in South Texas, I hear my southern accent sometimes and it scares me a little! Lol! I want you to know that being a woman of faith is not free of struggles nor is it always having a bold confident demeanor. Many times, it is just the opposite. Walking by faith is not easy. It is making a choice during a storm or storms. The good news is that through each storm, you are becoming stronger in the Lord and in the power of His might. There have been many dark times in my life that forced me to look up, focus on Jesus and learn to walk by faith and not by sight. My first forty years were filled with verbal, emotional, physical, mental, and spiritual abuse. Including four years of being stalked, and having our lives threatened along with the devastation of adultery, divorce and ultimately being abandoned. The result was a professional diagnosis of Post-Traumatic Stress Disorder, Panic/Anxiety Disorder with Depression. My desire is to overcome, not only for me, but for my children, and future generations to come. My goal in this chapter is to share what my fingerprint of faith looks like; and in the process help focus and fix your eyes on Jesus, the author, perfector and finisher of "Your Faith"!• Share with us what your business/ministry is and what it does for those that you serve.

My life and ministry are still developing. After many years of therapy, I can say: I'm a work in progress! One ministry is intercession through prayer, worship and dance. I can see some of your eyebrows raise, "dance?" yes dance! Before you jump off here, I hope you will continue to read and be encouraged that God is in the business of fulfilling His Word! In the late 90's amid great sorrow, He turned my mourning into dancing! (Psalm 30:11

AMPC). I learned to worship God in spirit and in truth while dancing to Christian worship songs. Many people have asked how I can still be smiling while going through such intense circumstances. I can most assuredly say it's because God fulfilled this scripture and turned my morning into dancing because of the precious joy of His Presence. When you worship, He shows up! It's that simple. By His direction, I created and directed a youth dance team, where we preached the gospel through dance and interceded for others in prayer. During this time, I realized God had created and called me to this purpose and I love it! I received many reports of those touched by God in a special way as we ministered through dance. People would say they "heard the message" while we danced. So, Interesting! So cool what God can do! This public ministry was put on hold by devastating circumstances. I realize now that I did not have the foundation to sustain any ministry long term. Since then, God has been building a firm and immovable foundation. He has taught me important things about His character, His nature and His love. Lessons regarding the pitfalls of people pleasing and most important of all, walking by faith and not by sight! My heart yearns for the hurting and the lost. Through His great love I have seen many answered prayers, miracles of provision, mercy, grace and love, not just for me, but for those I have prayed for. I have seen others receive Christ and their lives transformed. The messy, but beautiful inward work only He can do. He wants an All Access Pass, to our mind, will and emotions, He needs our agreement and willingness to allow Him to reshape us and our lives into His image.

DIRECTION - Sometimes people are confused in recognizing and knowing what they are called to do by the Lord. What advice would you share in how one can hear and know what God has called them to do?

Gifts and talents from God flow freely and are a natural part of who you are! They are things you absolutely love to do and when you operate in those gifts and talents you feel whole and fulfilled. Many people try to shut down their gifts, thinking they must give them up as a sacrifice for God, this is incorrect teaching. God gave us our gifts and talents to glorify Him and to build up the body of Christ, so we may be strong and work together in unity, reaching out as Jesus did to the hopeless, the poor, the widows, the orphans, the sick and more. These are acts of worship and faith in action!

DIRECTION – There are times when someone may struggle with really knowing their gifts and how to use them. How did you know what you were gifted in, and how do you apply that in your life?

It took time to realize intercessory prayer was a spiritual gift. Dance, intercessory dance was a gift I never saw coming. I still can't wrap my mind around it. It's totally through the Holy Spirit and the Word of God. When pregnant with my youngest son, I found myself going through that pregnancy alone, with 2 other children at home. My heart was completely shattered and my children's too. A home group at church took us in and prayed for me and my children unceasingly, showering us with love and support. Through this group, I began to experience the love of God for the very 1st time. At 35 and a Christian for most of my life, I had heard God loved me, I was certain He loved others, but I didn't really know if He loved me, because I hated me. They showed me His love through human acts of acceptance, kindness, unconditional love, support, encouragement and a few of them gave endless hours of time and attention, something I had never known. They made Jesus real to me. As I began to open to receive their love, one morning during worship at church I was able to open and receive the most beautiful love I had ever experienced. I didn't know love like that even existed, it was Jesus and He loved me with a transforming love and I have never been the same. His love helps me in everything I do and everywhere I go no matter what is happening! I said all of that to say, I am a late bloomer. I am becoming aware of my gifts and talents. I now know, I am an encourager, I have the gift of mercy and grace. The gift of dance, in the natural I am very uncoordinated and clumsy. I never had dance lessons, yet some of our youth who had, would tell me the name of different ballet moves that I was doing. I had no earthly knowledge of this. It came from spending much time in the Word of God and worshipping Him in spirit and in truth as His word says. It's amazing that He will give you gifts and talents you don't naturally have. How fun is that!

DIRECTION - Many people struggle with developing a habit of including God in all that they do. How do you make God a part of your life/business/ministry each day?

He is the most important part of me! If you have invited him into your heart and your life, He dwells within you and is constantly with you! I consult Him on everything. In my twenties, I read a little book that helped shape my faith called "The Practice of the Presence of God" by Brother Lawrence. It's about practicing the presence of God in everything you do, whether it's important or menial, even when sleeping. The title of the booklet is perfect because it does takes practice. A conscious effort, especially when all hell is breaking loose. Practice knowing that God is there and seeing Jesus during the storms, because He is. Practice every day, like pumping irons, and build your faith muscle. During life, it's by faith that we walk, standing on God's word, trusting He is faithful even when we are not. He promises to work all things out for our good, because we love Him! We must give him time to do this.

FAITH - As a woman of faith, what has been your biggest obstacle or challenge in your faith walk with God, and how did you navigate that successfully?

It's hard to pick one, there have been so many. Let's start at the beginning, when I was young. I had a recurring nightmare that terrified me. I was always being chased by three white giants while running for my life, it was so real. Interestingly, my life has always felt like that. Over time, I understood there were three major giants that were blinding me from receiving all God had for me. Suddenly, in 2014, I heard God say, "It's time to face your giants". I was ready! David and Goliath kept coming to mind, so I began reading the story in the Word and it came alive! Things I had never noticed before took on new meaning. I had never understood the Old Testament and now it was alive, relevant and exciting! Since I can remember, I was plagued by a debilitating, paralyzing fear that circumstances made worse. The Lord showed me in 1995, that if I could allow Him to turn all my fear into faith, there is nothing I would not see! I was so excited! I know that day will come, we are making progress! I must choose faith every day during every circumstance, even amid debilitating, shaking, paralyzing fear! The first giant: fear/terror.

In 2014, upon my youngest son's graduation from high school, child support also ended. He graduated from high school with a 4.5 GPA and received a scholarship to Penn State and The University of Arkansas, with acceptance into the School of Architecture, only 50-60 students were accepted into each program. My son is also a gifted and anointed artist and competitive figure skater. His future was bright. We began to struggle financially without the child support and I was struggling with an illness. My son didn't have to, but he chose to put his life, education and dreams on hold, and went to work full time to help keep a roof over our head. He was heartbroken and so was I, for him. My son chose to walk by faith. We were engulfed in many trials and tests for the next two years. It felt like we were in the deepest darkest part of the ocean, drowning, with no light in sight. Thoughts of suicide began to haunt both of us. Just when it seemed we might have a breakthrough from 2 years of hell, I broke my back, an L4 compression fracture.

My son now had to do everything for me. I was in blinding pain, with the wrong medication blinding my mind. Our dog passed away. A few months later through a set of circumstances, I found myself alone; desperation, hopelessness and depression began to set in. All I felt from those I loved was abandonment, judgment and contempt, which I couldn't even process at the time. It broke me. Yet, in that blinding darkness, loneliness and pain, He was there. Unexpectedly, God did some Red Sea miracles of provision through several people. One day, a song came on the radio, the words of this song pierced through years of darkness! The song was "Just be Held" by Casting Crowns. It became my lifeline! I held onto every word. It seemed to be a message God had written to me at the exact moment my world completely fell apart and I really needed to just be held.

Through a series of circumstances, a surprise ticket was given to me by Jen at KSBJ Radio to a Casting Crowns concert in my area. I received so much internal healing at the concert that it changed the trajectory of my life! As that time of miraculous provision closed, my faith was tested and tried to my core. In August of 2017 in the heat of Texas, I had no home, nowhere to go; no funds and I could not work due to my health. God was all I had left. I realize now that the circumstances were by His design; we had another giant to face. I grew up in the projects-an empty refrigerator many times and now I was facing being homeless, with nowhere to go, no provision in site, and still in horrific physical and emotional pain. Terror was again kicking in the door. After much prayer, I can confidently say, the second giant: Could I trust God to take care of me, when I couldn't? The answer: Yes! Amazingly! Beyond all I could ask, think or imagine!

At the end of October 2017, I got a virus that took me the rest of the way out. I was hospitalized, twice and began intense therapy again. The day after Christmas, with no fight left in me, suicide began to relentlessly beat down the door of my soul for the last time. It was way too strong for me, I knew only God could help me, whatever it was, was deeply rooted. I was losing this battle, it was about to win and take my life. I knew if God didn't help me, I wasn't going to make it. Whatever this was had affected every area and relationship in my life, even my walk with God. I terrifyingly gave Him permission to this area in my heart. I desperately wanted God to do whatever it took for me to move forward in life and into all that He had for me. I really didn't know what had caused this thing that terrified my entire being. It wasn't until after He had slain this giant that He showed me, "the third giant: Abandonment". Through prayer and counseling the Lord revealed I had been an unwanted pregnancy. Most of my 57 years I had felt unwanted and unloved, and circumstances always seemed to confirm it. Truth be known, by this time, I didn't want me either. I had been fighting thoughts of suicide off and on for about three years, but on December 26th of 2017, I was forced to decide. Would I live and allow God to do what He wanted to in my life? Or would I give up? Give in? I was tired, so very tired of fighting for my life, my entire life. The desperation of the feelings of abandonment were so strong, it seemed I had no choice but to drive off the bridge that day; it was overtaking me. As I cried out to the Lord, I heard Him say with great clarity, "It's your choice, you can choose". Not really what I wanted or expected to hear. But it was the truth! IT WAS MY CHOICE! My response,

"Lord, I choose you, enable me". To the left would have been death, and as strong as that pull was, I somehow turned right across four lanes into a parking lot and cried incessantly, talking to God about how much I hurt. I was raw to the core, I couldn't breathe. I was exhausted from the fight of choosing to live, but not really wanting to. I was at my end, I had no fight left. Three days later on Friday, I went to church. I got there early. I walked in the door and sat down, the music began to play; it was the song I had ministered through dance in 1999. "Breathe, you are the Air I breathe" and immediately the healing presence of God was so warm in the center of my being; filling this gaping, gnawing hole and it felt so good! I couldn't really move or talk much for the next 3 hours! You see, with my choice, He was able to reach into the deepest part of my soul, hidden through muck and mire and uproot the lie of abandonment and slay that giant! I was wanted! He wanted me, I was His idea! Where the weeds of abandonment and all its branches of lies were woven throughout my heart, He extracted them and left only the Truth of His Word that I had stored up in my heart for years. Something only an excellent surgeon could do. He touched me and made me whole! I am forever changed, because now I know He will never abandon me! Nor will He will abandon you! Never! (Hebrews 13:5 AMPC)

FAITH – Many people struggle with having faith when things around them seem to go awry. What would you advise someone who wants to strengthen their faith?

Press in to Jesus and His Word! It's impossible to have faith in someone you don't know. A person is known by their character, integrity and motives. Jesus Christ is the most beautiful, loving, amazing person I know! Jesus said if you have seen me, you have seen the Father. Knowing the truths of God's Word is one thing, walking them out by faith is another. Believing that God will do what He says He will do, in His timing, is the key to walking by faith while believing He has your best interest at heart. If God hasn't taken you out of a hard season, then He has a good reason. I've heard it said that setbacks are a setup for God to show up and show out. I can say I have seen this played out in my life many times over. It is true, if we seek God and obey Him in the setback, we can watch Him do the impossible! It is His specialty! Our "choice" is the most important weapon we have besides the Word of God. Ask the Holy Spirit to enable you to walk by faith, enable you to choose, and enable you to receive! We overcome by the Blood of the Lamb and the Word of our testimony (Rev 12:11 NKJV), meaning the Word of God coming through our choice, mind and mouth!

OVERCOME - How do you structure your time to reflect all the priorities and opportunities God has given you to be a light for him without losing yourself in the process, both personally and professionally?

If I lose Him, I lose me. I am now so intertwined and interdependent upon Him, His presence, His Holy Spirit and His Word, I can't exist without Him! I used to get scared when I couldn't spend time with Him, or feel His presence, scared He would leave. I don't worry about that now because it isn't true. He never leaves us; His Word says so! It took years of getting to know Him and His word to get this truth, but it doesn't have to take you years! He wants a relationship with you more than you do with Him! He's waiting for you always!

OVERCOME - Share with us about a season in your life that God sent you through that changed the course of your life.

There have been many seasons that have changed my course and taught me who God is and how to walk by faith. I have grown closer

to Him in the process. I see His character, which builds my faith and trust in Him as He brings me through each storm. I just came through the darkest season of my life; it lasted four years altogether. I had to learn to "let go and let God". I am now able to love myself, something I've never been able to do. I am still tested in this area, but my foundation of faith is stronger than ever. I'm convinced now, more than ever, that God is willing and able. The question is, am I? Our participation with the Holy Spirit is key to growing spiritually!
• POUR -What three scriptures would you share with someone if they are in a season of transition and need clarity? Also, share why you selected these three scriptures.

It is important to know that seasons are temporary, not permanent and God has a work He wants to do in you through it! Nothing is permanent unless we give up or quit. Every day I must choose who I will serve; Fear? Man? Anger? My flesh? The enemy? Or, will I serve; God? Forgiveness? Peace, Righteousness? Joy? Faith in God and not what I see? Work with His Holy Spirit; agree with God's Word, His Will, and His Way. His plans for you are for good and not for evil, to give you a future and a hope, a purpose, and a plan for you that is way beyond anything you can ask, think or imagine. Let him grow your faith, so when He gives you His best, nothing can take it away! Jeremiah 29:11, Ephesians 3:20

POUR -What is your favorite scripture, and how has that influenced your role as a woman who works and walks by faith?

He makes a way where there is no way (Isaiah 43:16 mine). The circumstances I have faced in the past and today, as I write, are looking to the Lord to make a way where there is no way. The more I walk through these impossible circumstances and see Him part the waters before me and close the water on the giants behind me, my faith and trust in Him builds. It doesn't mean I don't feel fear, terror at times or struggle with doubt, or insecurities, I must "choose" and keep going. When I can't hold on anymore, He holds me, and He will hold you! I count on Him to carry me through until the day I meet Him in glory!

Any closing thoughts?

Faith requires Focus. Focus on Jesus, the author and perfector and finisher of your faith. He can guide you through the journey of your life, teaching you how to exercise faith when, where and how during the storms. I believe every person's journey of faith, is like a fingerprint. No two fingerprints are alike; no two journeys of faith are the same either. Your journey is your own. I like to call it your "Fingerprint of Faith"; uniquely yours intertwined with others at points of time throughout your life as needed. Faith is not something you have to muster up, it is given to you when you believe in Jesus Christ and invited Him into your heart and life as your savior and friend. This is the first and most important act of faith! How beautiful! Faith is a journey, a lifelong journey. As the storms get bigger, so does the opportunity to leave your fingerprint of faith on the mark of that storm. It's hard work, but it gets easier the more you practice and stand on the word of God! Don't give up, persevere until the end. Run your race, finish your course with the help of the Holy Spirit. God never gives up on you. Don't give up on Him. And as I am learning, never give up on yourself. All Praise Be to God.

The Just Shall Live by Their Faith
Galatians 3:11, Romans 1:17, Habakkuk 2:4…

RACHEL BAILEY

Tell us a little about yourself.

I grew up going to church every Sunday and yet, I always saw God as more of a cosmic killjoy than a good Father. For years, I tried to find life in sex, alcohol, parties, and stuff but it left me empty, anxious, and depressed. A friend invited me to a young adults' ministry where God opened my heart and I understood the Gospel for the first time. Since then, God has radically transformed my life, even if it is sometimes slower than I would like. He has used His Spirit, His Word, and His people to mold me consistently into the image of His Son. I, along with everyone else, am still far from perfection. I have insecurities. I desperately want the approval of others. Sometimes I stress when the illusion of control is taken from me. I struggle to believe that God really loves me. I could name fifty more, but the point is God has given me plenty to trust Him with every minute. I have served with preschoolers as well as young adults and I love both. I truly believe God is going to do big things with my generation (millennials) and I'm excited to play a small part in His plan. My heart is to help people go from a lukewarm, Sunday-only religion to a life-giving relationship with Jesus.

Share with us what your business/ministry is and what it does for those that you serve.

Right now, I'm in school getting a degree in leadership and ministry. I would love a teaching role with women or possibly youth. We'll see what the Lord has in store, though. His plan is always better!

I'm a member of The Village Church where I serve in Connections as well as the preschool ministry, Little Village. In Connections, my job is to help people feel welcome in our church.

What we do is greet people help them find seats and have conversations. Despite the negative stereotype of people wanting churches to be cool, I have found that warmth is far more desired. I have learned that people want authentic human interaction more than good music and funny preaching. What drew me to both churches where I've been a member is their genuine interest in me and my relationship with the Lord. Serving in Connections is not just a chance to say "hi" to people. Rather, it is an opportunity to form relationships with others in the church, especially those coming for the first time. In Little Village, I have the super fun "job" of working with the largest group of unbelievers in our church. We play with them, pray for them, teach them Bible stories, and show them the love of Jesus. As much as it does for the little ones, it probably does more for my own heart. My love and delight in these precious kids despite their total dependency on me and inability to do anything for me is a beautiful picture of the way our relationship to God is. To think He loves us like a father loves a child is beyond our comprehension and it's one of the most profound truths of scripture.

DIRECTION - Sometimes people are confused in recognizing and knowing what they are called to do by the Lord. What advice would you share in how one can hear and know what God has called them to do?

There are a few passages of Scripture I would go to for an answer to this. One is 1 Corinthians 12:7-10 where Paul says, "To each is given the manifestation of the Spirit for the common good. For to one is given through the Spirit the utterance of wisdom, and to another the utterance of knowledge according to the same Spirit, to another faith by the same Spirit, to another gifts of healing by the one Spirit, to another the working of miracles, to another prophecy, to another the ability to distinguish between spirits, to another various kinds of tongues, to another the interpretation of tongues." Another passage is Acts 17:26-27 that says "And [God] made from one man every nation of mankind to live on all the face of the earth, having determined allotted periods and the boundaries of their dwelling place, that they should seek God, and perhaps feel their way toward him and find him. Yet he is actually not far from each one of us."

In trying to recognize what God has called us to do, there are two questions we can ask based on these verses. What are my gifts and how can I use them where I am right now? Paul clearly states that it is God who gives us our gifts. Do we have room to grow and mature in them? Absolutely but we must first be empowered by the Spirit. The second passage tells us that God has determined when and where we will live. That means that even if we are discontent with where we are right now, God knows exactly what He is doing in our lives. Shouldn't that alone shift our perspective? I don't have to move somewhere else or find a different job to live out God's calling on my life. I have a purpose where I am right now. I think we all, in our limited knowledge, can sometimes get too caught up in God's specific calling for us. We shouldn't stress about what ministry we will serve or what career God wants us to work. Jesus tells us in Matthew 28:19-20 that His calling for all of us is to "Go therefore and make disciples of all nations, baptizing them in the name of the Father and of the Son and of the Holy Spirit, teaching them to observe all that I have commanded you." He has already revealed His calling for us in Scripture. We live it out using our unique gifts where He has sovereignly placed us for His glory and our joy.

DIRECTION – There are times when someone may struggle with really knowing their gifts and how to use them. How did you know what you were gifted in, and how do you apply that in your life?

This is one place where living in community and being known by others becomes so important. When you "do life" with people for any amount of time, they can start to notice things you're gifted in and help you grow in those gifts. Another thing that has proved helpful in my life is jumping in and serving somewhere. I didn't know I had the gift of hospitality until I started serving on the greeting team at my old church. I didn't really know I had a teaching gift until I started leading a small group and went on a mission trip where I was given the opportunity to teach. Therefore, being plugged into a church, as opposed to just attending, is important. We should not be consumers but active members. Find some areas in your church that need help and pray about where God might have you step in. Finally, I'm almost hesitant to share this because it's more of a supplement than an answer but there are an online spiritual gifts tests that can be helpful. My small group took our tests together and went over the answers to see how accurate they were. We should always do things in the context of community. While an internet test is helpful, it shouldn't be an excuse to not let others speak into our lives.

DIRECTION - Many people struggle with developing a habit of including God in all that they do. How do you make God a part of your life/business/ministry each day?

One word—discipline. There is no silver bullet or quick fix that will transport the Bible into your brain each day (though that would be awesome). Let's all admit it. Sometimes it is hard to want to spend time with the Lord. Sometimes we don't feel like praying.

Sometimes we don't want to enter the awkwardness of a conversation about faith. Spiritual warfare is a real thing and the enemy will do whatever he can to distract us from God. He will tempt us with lesser things to keep us from enjoying our greatest treasure. I'm certainly not perfect in this and there have been more times than I care to admit where I will choose watching a show or scrolling through Facebook instead of reading my Bible or talking to God. Something that has been helpful to me is to think about times in your day when you have an extra couple minutes and use that time to pray. For me, I get a lot of praying done driving to work or even while I'm showering. It doesn't have to (and probably won't) be super romantic with a beautiful sunrise and the quietness of a morning with the Holy Spirit personally coming to you in visible form. I try to wake up 20-30 minutes early each day to pray and read my Bible. I also try to have some extended prayer time before going to bed. Outside of that, it's a lot of short prayers throughout the day. Another thing that really helps me is I almost always have worship music playing. Letting your mind absorb that truth helps set your heart on the things of God and be more mindful of Him and His purpose for you throughout the day. Lastly, we all need community to encourage us, admonish us, and keep us accountable. We will all pursue God imperfectly, but He has given us one another as a means of grace in our lives.

FAITH - As a woman of faith, what has been your biggest obstacle or challenge in your faith walk with God, and how did you navigate that successfully?

As a relatively young believer, I can honestly say the biggest challenge in my faith is happening right now. I've been truly blessed to have been a member at two amazing churches since becoming a Christian. Both have fostered cultures of love and authenticity where "it's okay to not be okay." Despite that, there is a deep-rooted fear in my heart that if I'm fully honest about my struggles, my weaknesses, the places where I am NOT okay, then nobody will love me. The enemy has subtly and powerfully used shame in my life to try to "steal and kill and destroy" (John 10:10). My biggest obstacle has been my own sin of not being completely honest with myself, with God, and especially with other people. The approval of others has always been an idol for me. It used to look like finding my worth in men and being the life of the party. Now it looks like serving in the right ministries, reading the right books, listening to the right pastors, and memorizing the right verses. All those things are good things. However, in many instances, my heart yearned more for people to approve of me versus God's approval. It is such a subtle shift that it's hard to notice without Spirit-empowered introspection. In the misplaced desire for others to like or love me, I projected all my strengths and hid all my weaknesses. If we're honest, that is something a lot, if not all, of us do. We put on a mask and pretend everything is great. We believe the lie that if we pretend to be more than we are, people will love us.

Ironically, it is that pretending that keeps people from loving us. To be fully loved, we must be fully known. The funny thing is I can't tell you how many sermons I've listened to and books I've read that shared that. Intellectually, I know vulnerability is freeing. Yet, it wasn't until the last couple months that I've really experienced the consequences of constantly wearing a mask. It has made me feel isolated, alone, and depressed. To say I've successfully navigated it feels like a stretch since I'm currently wrestling through it. However, I have been committed to being fully honest with God (since He already knows anyway) and with those close to me and it has been a freeing and healing experience. It is important to be reminded of the Gospel every single day. God does not love a future version of us any more than He loves and delights in us right now. It was at our worst when He saved us! It's His love and grace that enables us to be who we are, weakness and all, so that His glory and strength will be shown through us.

FAITH – Many people struggle with having faith when things around them seem to go awry. What would you advise someone who wants to strengthen their faith?

There's a line in a song by Rend Collective that says, "what's true in the light is still true in the dark." When we're going through good seasons of life, we tend to forget that we need to pursue God just as relentlessly. However, I have found that many of the peace-giving truths and promises I cling to in the rough season I'm in right now, are ones that I learned and studied when things were going well. Simple truths like; God is good, and God is in total control are easy to believe when things are going my way. When everything falls apart, it becomes difficult. It's even more difficult if I'm digging into my Bible to find these promises. No matter where you are when you're reading this, my advice is the same—read your Bible. The Bible is great because it's honest, it's messy, and it's true. Giants of the faith like Abraham and Moses greatly doubted God's sovereignty and goodness. Yet, God always has a plan even if it rarely, if ever, matches up with ours. Search the Word for His promises, pray for the faith to believe them, and surround yourself with others who can mourn with you while still reminding you of the hope and victory that is inevitably yours in Christ.

OVERCOME - How do you structure your time to reflect all the priorities and opportunities God has given you to be a light for him without losing yourself in the process, both personally and professionally?

It can be really challenging to find a balance. As Christians, we want to be stewards of our time and resources to be a light where we are. We also don't want to get so caught up in "doing" that we forget to be still before the Lord and let Him work in us and through us. I've really learned, and am still learning, by trial and error. I've gone through a couple seasons where I overcommitted myself and felt like I was just going through the motions. I've also gone through seasons where I chose my own comfort rather than living out what God has called me to. It's hard to find a balance but a balance can be found. There're obvious things that are a part of my life like work, small group, school, and CrossFit. God uses me in each of those places in unique ways. Outside of that, I can figure out how much time I realistically have and choose a place to serve from there. I serve once a month with Connections and every week of every other month with Little Village. I'm also mentoring a girl through a recovery program. These things put together allow me plenty of opportunities for disciple-making while also investing in my own relationship with the Lord.

OVERCOME - Share with us about a season in your life that God sent you through that changed the course of your life.

It's difficult to name just one because when I look back, I can see how God has really used every season to shape the course of my life. I love seeing how God has worked in my heart through various circumstances. The hard but true reality is that the seasons we grow the most are the ones in which we are most desperate for Him. For me, that time is right now. If you would have asked me two months ago where I would be at the end of this year, I would have told you I'd be married and hopefully in an internship position at my church. God, in His mercy, blew all that up. I mentioned earlier some of the dark areas of my heart that God revealed to me in the last couple months. Things that I have been suppressing for years were suddenly in front of me. All my relationships had been affected and I was too prideful to even notice. After lots of prayer and conversations with community, I broke off the relationship I was in, joined a recovery program at my church, and started biblical counseling. The Lord showed me that before I fill my schedule with ministry activities and before I commit my life to someone, He had some healing to do in my heart. During all my doing, He wanted me to be still and trust Him. I don't know how long it's going to take but I think I've learned my lesson to not rush. God's timing is perfect, and His ways are infinitely higher than mine. My year is already looking nothing like I had planned. I was running full-speed in the wrong direction and I'm grateful that He loves me enough to break my legs.

POUR -What three scriptures would you share with someone if they are in a season of transition and need clarity? Also, share why you selected these three scriptures.

The first scripture I would use is James 1:5 that says, "If any of you lacks wisdom, let him ask God, who gives generously to all without reproach, and it will be given him." This is the most important one to me because it's a guarantee. If you ask God for wisdom, He will give it. Parents, when your kid asks you for help, do you not delight to give it to them? Isn't it even more so with our perfect Heavenly Father? The next one I would share is 2 Timothy 3:16 that says, "All Scripture is breathed out by God and profitable for teaching, for reproof, for correction, and for training in righteousness." This one might seem strange, but I chose it because it emphasizes the importance of our bibles. God speaks to us through His Word. Even if you don't have clarity on a specific situation like a job transition, a relationship or anything that would fall in God's unrevealed will, He does have a lot to say in His revealed will. Rest in His promises and obey His commands and it will go well with you. Finally, I would use 1 Corinthians 10:31 which says "So, whether you eat or drink, or whatever you do, do all to the glory of God." This verse should help us stop navel-gazing and remember what's important. We are living in a story far bigger than any of us can imagine. No matter where we are in life, our purpose and drive should be the same—to bring glory to our Father.

POUR -What is your favorite scripture, and how has that influenced your role as a woman who works and walks by faith?

My favorite Scripture is Psalms 115:3 that says, "Our God is in the heavens; he does all that he pleases." It's simple yet it says so much. When we take into consideration the nature and character of God (His goodness, kindness, mercy, love, grace, compassion), this verse becomes the warmest blanket to our soul. My God, who knows and loves me fully, is in total control over everything. No matter what happens in my life, God is sovereign over it. He doesn't send me through hard times to punish me, but to draw me closer to Him. When I trust that God is good, that He loves me and that He does all that He pleases, I can truly have peace. I don't have to know all the answers because I know and trust the One that does. To quote Jonathan Edwards, "Absolute sovereignty is what I love to ascribe to God."

Any closing thoughts?

My hope for all women in their Christian walk is that they would drink deeply from the inexhaustible well that is our God. Don't be satisfied with cute devotionals and Proverbs 31. Don't get me wrong, those are great. However, there is much more joy to be had. Study the Old Testament. Get some theology books. Sign up for an equipping class at your church. Listen to podcasts. The more we know God, the more we will trust and love Him. The security I have in the season I'm in right now comes from years of building a solid foundation on which to stand. Don't think the more in-depth material is only for men. God created us equal but distinct. Women have unique minds and hearts that the church needs to flourish. May we not get to the end of our lives and realized we wasted it on ourselves. If we want abundant life, it is only found in treasuring Jesus Christ and using our lives to make much of Him.

TEREE
WARREN

Tell us a little about yourself.

I was raised in the Washington, DC area where my mom and sister currently reside. I have been blessed to have had opportunities to live in California, Kentucky, Wisconsin and Texas. Each of those moves had lasting, positive impacts on my life and molded me into the person that I am today. I have been working in the field of Forensic Science, analyzing seized drugs, for almost 11 years. I have been a member of my church for ten years, where I have served on several auxiliaries and as the church administrator.

Share with us what your business/ministry is and what it does for those that you serve.

My ministry primarily consists of church administration, teaching, intercession and encouragement. As church administrator I assist the senior pastors in managing the organizational structure and supporting auxiliaries of the church. As a teacher I help to ground believers in the word of God - taking difficult concepts and teaching them in a way that everyone can understand. As an intercessor I pray for God's will to be done in the earth and for others to receive their breakthrough and blessing. As an encourager I provide comfort and cheer to the discouraged, downcast and downtrodden. In all that I do, it is my godly desire for people to know Christ and recognize who they are in God.

DIRECTION - Sometimes people are confused in recognizing and knowing what they are called to do by the Lord. What advice would you share in how one can hear and know what God has called them to do?

First, I would get to know God not for what He can do, but for who He is to you. As He reveals more about Himself, He reveals more about you. This process can provide the healing necessary to open your heart to God's possibilities and not man's. Second, I would begin to ask God to use you and let Him know that you are available to be used. Third, I would pray that God shows you how He sees you. Last, I would ask God to reveal a scripture supporting your calling - one to stand on in turbulent times.

One thing to remember is not to overthink during this process. We can think that because we see certain callings in operation in the church that we too must operate in those calls. This is not true for everyone. There are those who are meant to only operate within the four walls of the church or the marketplace and those that operate in both.

DIRECTION – There are times when someone may struggle with really knowing their gifts and how to use them. How did you know what you were gifted in, and how do you apply that in your life?

It took me a long time to know and accept my gifts because I suffered from low self-esteem. I experienced a lot of rejection in my youth that caused me to second guess and not understand my true value. It became very difficult to see the good in me through the negativity that had been spoken over me. But through God's grace I was able to see myself as He sees me.

Finding your gifting can be as simple as walking down memory lane. Ask yourself what is your passion, how has your passion affected others around you and can it bring glory to God? After you have answered those three questions then it is time to seek God through prayer, fasting and the word. Your answer will usually come in two ways - heavenly affirmation and earthly confirmation. Your heavenly affirmation may come through the word of God - a prophetic utterance, shared words of wisdom or knowledge, scripture, preached message, or any combination of the five. Your earthly confirmation may come through someone you least expect - a stranger, coworker or someone who has no personal knowledge of your 'quest.'

During this process you can try different things to discover your gifting even if you find they are not for you.

DIRECTION - Many people struggle with developing a habit of including God in all that they do. How do you make God a part of your life/business/ministry each day?

This is still a struggle of mine; however, I am growing. The first thing I had to do is set my mind for discipline. The truth is that we make time for the things we truly want to do. We are disciplined in so many areas even when we think that we aren't - the time that we wake up in the morning, eat lunch, watch our favorite TV show, and go to bed. I had to decide to operate in discipline to spend time with God in prayer, reading the word, listening to Christian music and preaching.

With any type of discipline, it's best to start small and be consistent. Set reasonable goals. Start with something you know you can achieve and then increase that incrementally. My favorite time to spend with God is in the car on my commutes to work and church. Also, do not be so hard on yourself when you miss the mark. Just pick back up where you left off and keep on going. Remember that

God wants to hear about your day just as much as a spouse or a best friend, if not more.

FAITH - As a woman of faith, what has been your biggest obstacle or challenge in your faith walk with God, and how did you navigate that successfully?

The biggest obstacle in my faith walk has been being "a make it happen woman." On the surface this can be an admirable quality; however, it can also be contrary to faith. When God speaks a promise to me, I immediately try to figure out the how. I plan and then begin to execute it. This has made it difficult for me to get out of God's way and allow Him to move as He so desires. I have learned the hard way that eventually God will allow us to try to no avail. This can be a heartbreaking process and at times has made me want to give up on the promise completely.

I have learned that there is a level of surrender that I had to reach to allow God to work a work in me and in my situation to bring about the promise. The surrender required me to fast, pray, and release the burden of trying to make things happen for myself. I had to ask myself some difficult questions like why I felt the need to make things happen instead of letting God have His way. I had to heal from trust issues with people that ultimately carried over into my relationship with God. I learned that there are times when God wants us to drive and times when He wants us to sit back and let Him drive. I also learned that I had to be sensitive enough to the Holy Spirit to know the difference.

FAITH – Many people struggle with having faith when things around them seem to go awry. What would you advise someone who wants to strengthen their faith?

One practical thing to do is write down the word that God gives you, then go back and write the date of performance. Keep this in a journal or notebook as a reminder that God can and will fulfill His promises to you.

The important principle is to always go back to the word of God. God does everything decent and in order. We never go through a test without instructions from our instructor. God will always give us a word to stand on before our trial. This word can come in various forms, it can be a preached word, word of wisdom, knowledge, scripture or even a song. The best thing is to soak in this word. Speak it daily, post it around your home, play the song multiple times. You must have some sort of reminder that your current situation is temporary and that the word of God will always prevail.

OVERCOME - How do you structure your time to reflect all the priorities and opportunities God has given you to be a light for him without losing yourself in the process, both personally and professionally?

Say it with me balance. B-A-L-A-N-C-E. This is something that I still struggle with. I have the hardest time choosing one thing over another. It always brings up feelings of guilt, that I am letting one group down to help another. Recently I have come to the realization that I am my most valuable resource. If I don't take the time out to nourish, take care of and honor me then I am no good to the Kingdom of God. We must first honor God, take care of ourselves, family and then ministry. If there is no you, then there is no reason for priorities or opportunities to come to you.

OVERCOME - Share with us about a season in your life that God sent you through that changed the course of your life.

I graduated college in 2007 when the American economy was on the brink of what we now know as the Great Recession. It was my desire to work for a certain agency but there were hiring freezes all over the Washington, DC area at that time. My mom and I decided that to start my career I was going to have to move away for a few years. That summer I worked at a veterinarian clinic to save up for the impending move. I filled out applications for three different states - Texas, Montana and Wisconsin. As I dropped the envelopes off at the post office, I prayed that God would emphatically show me which place I was to move. He did. I only received one response - Wisconsin.

Three weeks before my start date, my car's transmission went out. I had to make a choice, the car or my future. I chose the latter. By faith I moved to Milwaukee, Wisconsin with four bags on a 24hr bus ride the Thursday before Labor Day Weekend. I spent the next two days searching all over town for an apartment. I found one on Saturday, moved in on Sunday and started my new job on Tuesday.

Two months into my lease, the landlord was robbed at gunpoint and I knew I had to move. I searched for a place and found one. God granted me favor with the landlord, "because he liked my story," and held the apartment for me for two months until I could move. I had such a sense of victory as I went to sleep in my new place. The next morning, I awoke to the news that my grandmother had passed away in Maryland. In a new place - I grieved alone.

For the next few months I would hear church music three days a week coming from across the street - Sundays, Wednesdays and Thursdays. The funny thing is there were three churches across the street. As the weeks went by I managed to narrow it down to two that were side by side. Finally, one Sunday morning I decided to go to church. On my way across the street I asked God for three things: 1) that the pastor(s) would be like the church I grew up in, 2) there would be many members in my age group, and 3) there would be a single's ministry. The church I thought started at 11:00am started at 11:30am. I knew myself well enough that if I walked back across the street to my home, I would not be back. I walked into the church that started at 11:00am. Not only had each of my requests been granted, but I soon discovered this was the church that I had heard the music three days a week for six months.

It was at that church that I discovered that God had a purpose and plan for my life. God used the pastors to preach words of deliverance, healing, faith, strength and encouragement to build me up. It was in Wisconsin that I discovered my gifts and began to operate in them. It was at that church that I became the church administrator, teacher, intercessor and encourager that I was created to be.

Years later I realized that the very first time I had heard the church music was in the background as I was receiving the news of my grandmother's passing – Sunday, December 2, 2007 at 11:00am. God is truly faithful and orders the steps of the righteous. He always knows what we need and exactly when we need it.

POUR -What three scriptures would you share with someone if they are in a season of transition and need clarity? Also, share why you selected these three scriptures.

The three scriptures that I would share would be Joshua 1:8, Psalm 37:23, and Isaiah 43:19.

*This book of the law shall not depart out of thy
mouth; but thou shalt meditate therein day and night,
that thou mayest observe to do according to all that
is written therein: for then thou shalt make thy way
prosperous, and then thou shalt have good success.
(Joshua 1:8 KJV)*

Joshua 1:8 is powerful because it lets us know that a consistent intake of God's word is necessary during a season of transition. It is only through His word that our obedience to Him becomes easier and produces the fruit necessary to move forward into our season of promise.

*The steps of a good man are ordered by the Lord:
and he delighteth in his way. (Psalm 37:23 KJV)*

Psalm 37:23 because during a season of transition we can forget or think that God is no longer concerned with us. But this scripture tells us that no matter how unstable our life can be or feel during transition, God is still in control and actively ordering our steps.

*Behold, I will do a new thing; now it shall spring
forth; shall ye not know it? I will even make a way in
the wilderness, and rivers in the desert. (Isaiah 43:19
KJV)*

Isaiah 43:19 is a reminder of the power of God and how He can step into our situation in a moment's notice. It is also a reminder not to gauge the future by the present or even the past. Keep your mind open to receive the new thing(s) that He is doing.

POUR -What is your favorite scripture, and how has that influenced your role as a woman who works and walks by faith?

My absolute favorite scripture is Ephesians 3:20, but when it comes to faith I've had to stand on Romans 4:17-21, specifically verse 20.

[17](As it is written, I have made thee a father of many nations,) before him whom he believed, even God, who quickeneth the dead, and calleth those things which be not as though they were. [18]Who against hope believed in hope, that he might become the father of many nations; according to that which was spoken, So shall thy seed be. [19]And being not weak in faith, he considered not his own body now dead, when he was about an hundred years old, neither yet the deadness of Sara's womb: **[20]He staggered not at the promise of God through unbelief; but was strong in faith, giving glory to God;** *[21]And being fully persuaded that, what he had promised, he was able also to perform. (Romans 4:17-21 KJV, emphasis added)*

This scripture reminds me that God's promises may not come when we desire. During those times we cannot afford to agree with the unbelief, doubt and fear that will surely come. We must stand flat-footed on the promises of God and continue to give God the praise that He truly deserves. It is in that praise that we begin to elevate our God above our circumstances. This praise shifts the atmosphere in our favor producing one promised victory after another.

Any closing thoughts?

We have entered a season where God really wants to bless His people - internally and externally. This is the season where all dreams can come true. But the only way to truly embrace this season is by faith. According to Hebrews 11:1, "*Faith is the substance of things hoped for, the evidence of things not seen.*"

In this season our faith must be greater than our natural sight. In fact, as our natural sight sees opposition, it is our faith that will guide us into the blessing that we have not room enough to receive. We must be crazy enough to believe that the impossible can be possible with our God because He is a promise keeper.

TINA
PARMIGIANO

Tell us a little about yourself.

I was raised in a small country town in Oregon (360 pop.). My father was a pastor, which made me the local preacher's kid. I was the youngest of four and oh how we loved growing up in God's country. I loved singing solos in church on Sunday mornings and with my dad when he spoke at other churches to be the special singer. I grew up watching my parents set a great example of what being a Christian and striving to be more Christ-like really was. They were by no means perfect, but they tried to live a life devoted to following and sharing Jesus with everyone they met. Being the youngest, I had the loudest mouth and always wanting to be heard. I loved singing and was very outgoing. As I grew older, I have accomplished many things. I never got a college degree, but I do have a degree in the School of Hard Knocks. My life experiences have taught me to keep going, press on and keep the faith. I was a single mom at 22, my father passed away when I was 23 and life changed forever. I never had a problem getting a job and working, as I learned quickly. Fast forward, I am now married with four sons and 6.5 grandchildren. They are the loves of my life and excited to have number 7 arriving soon. I started my tax business about 20 yrs. ago while being a stay at home mom, living on a Navy Base. (My husband was in the military). Always doing something, I worked the most with direct sales companies. I am involved with several Christian women organizations and love doing whatever God calls me to do. I have taught women's bible studies, led women's ministry groups and on the worship team.

I am currently running my small tax business and going into coaching/consulting up and coming business owners and women who want and are stuck moving forward.

Share with us what your business/ministry is and what it does for those that you serve.

I have been a tax professional and business owner for more than 20 years. During that time, I have worked with all types of individuals and small businesses, growing both personally and professionally. Recently, I have also added in coaching and consulting and became a John Maxwell Team member and mentor. During this time in what I thought was just a business, God has taken me through many phases. As I look back, I was able to witness and pray with some of my clients. I serve in a way that I never thought I would. I help others see their financial situations, plan ways to keep them on top of what is financially going on in their businesses and even in their personal life. I also serve in a capacity at times of listening when they are hurting and need someone to talk to. To give an encouraging word or inspire them to keep going forward. Relationships are built in ways that God has used me to speak truth in love and to be the vessel for Him. I don't see my tax business being just about numbers and taxes, but about being able to help others in different ways as God leads. Now I am reaching out to women wanting to grow both personally and professionally. It's my way of giving back, sharing and encouraging others to move forward.

DIRECTION - Sometimes people are confused in recognizing and knowing what they are called to do by the Lord. What advice would you share in how one can hear and know what God has called them to do?

I think we have all been confused a time or two about what the Lord has called us to do. Personally, I have tossed and turned and overthought many times if I am where God wants me to be. Am I doing what I've really been called to do? Sometimes we are our own worst enemy with accepting that the position we are currently in is right where God wants us to be. I have been in the tax business for over 20 years and every year I say I am done, Lord I know you have something else for me to do, I don't want to do this anymore. I would feel God is calling me somewhere different, when really, it was me thinking I should be doing something different. I would end up with 10 to 20 new clients that year and it was when I stepped back, really looked at where I was, that I realized I was doing and working the talents in which God had given me. I had to learn to stop listening to myself or see what other women were doing in business and really listen to Him.

After that, the work became less frustrating and more interesting and worthwhile. It also brought me to new places, introduced new opportunities to grow personally and professionally and to help others do the same. It is amazing what happens when you let go and let God have His way. There is a lot of waiting and learning to trust in Him. That is why one of my favorites versus is Prov. 3:5,6...5) Trust in the Lord with all your heart and do not depend on your own understanding. 6)Seek his will in all you do, and he will show you which path to take." I put it this way..." I will trust in you Lord with all my heart and not on my own understanding. I will seek you first in all I do and then I know I am taking the right path." When I personalize scripture and read it out loud, it becomes real and a part of me. So, my advice is to stop and listen. What are you good at, what gifts or talents has God given you? If you are working with the talents He has given you, you are most likely doing what He is having you to do. He will let you know when the plan changes.

DIRECTION – There are times when someone may struggle with really knowing their gifts and how to use them. How did you know what you were gifted in, and how do you apply that in your life?

I used to ask that question all the time and sometimes I still wonder if I am really in the gift that God has for me. I always overthought what a "gift" really is, how does it look or act. It was after a lot of prayer and seeking God, seeking good counsel and listening to what was being said that God just opened my eyes one day to help me see that my gift went with my talents. I have the gift to encourage others, to make them laugh and lift them up. To serve others and build relationships. I do that in my business every day. There are "Spiritual Gift" assessments out there that you can take to help you narrow it down. I've taken both the "Spiritual Gifts Assessment" along with one based on strengths called "Strength Finder 2.0." On the spiritual gift side, my #1 gift was faith and in the other it was adaptability. As I look at these words, it is because of my faith, that I can be so adaptable. I've had to "Keep the Faith" so to speak in so many ways in my life. It has not been an easy road personally or professionally. I have had to face so many outside obstacles as well as self-inflicted hardships with doubt and fear that my faith was made stronger. From an early age I accepted Jesus into my heart and accepted the Bible as the complete and total truth, even though I did not understand a lot of it, I always knew it was true. Because of the faith in knowing I was never alone (even though at times I felt like I was) it kept me going. I was able to change and adapt to the circumstances and situations around me. As Paul said in Phil 4:12, 13 "I have learned to live on almost nothing or with everything. I have learned the secret of living in every situation, whether it is with a full stomach or empty, with plenty or little. 13)For I can do everything through Christ, who gives me strength."

DIRECTION - Many people struggle with developing a habit of including God in all that they do. How do you make God a part of your life/business/ministry each day?

It took me a long time to get into the habit of putting God first and making sure He was a big part of my day. To be honest, I went back and forth so many times in my life of diving deep into my bible study and prayer, teaching a study and putting Him on top. But then…life happened, and I got off track and stopped because of a family situation or something else. It took me a long time to realize I didn't have to push Him away when things weren't going right. But, the best part of my life is, is that God knows me. He knows my heart and knows that even in these unfocused, crazy, off the wall, I can do it myself or it is just too hard times, He brings me back to Him. I must work on it every single day. I can get off track at the blink of an eye and I am so thankful for a God that keeps me on track. Every morning before starting my day, I strive to do a daily devotional and pray. It doesn't have to long and drawn out, but I want to wake up and put God first in my mind. Feed my mind with the bread of life and allow to Him breathe life into me. Same thing for my business, He is my partner and CEO of my business. I consult with Him before making any major decisions and then take that step. If I end up taking the wrong step forward, He gently corrects me and sets me straight. Believe me, I have learned the hard way with this and now I don't want to go anywhere without God in the driver's seat. At the end of each evening before going to sleep, I spend a little quiet time with Him again, a short devotion or just reading in my bible and top my night off with prayer. Letting Him know just how thankful I am for another day to honor and glorify Him.

FAITH - As a woman of faith, what has been your biggest obstacle or challenge in your faith walk with God, and how did you navigate that successfully?

My biggest obstacle was myself and the challenge was changing my mindset. I had a hard time feeling I was good or smart enough. I listened to the devil so many times whisper in my ear, who do you think you are, you don't have any degrees...people won't trust you. I had to learn to believe in the woman God had created me to be. Besides, with Him, ALL things are possible, so if God called me to it, He will get me through it. The other was allowing outside distractions take over. When you are the only one walking with the Lord in your family, you get a phone call and it is your son saying he has been arrested and then to sit in a courtroom waiting to see if your son gets sentenced to 30 yrs. in prison. All the thoughts that go through your mind. Where did I go wrong? How could God let this happen to me? How am I ever going to get through this? Am I being punished for the things I did wrong long ago? But none of this is a punishment, they are the trials of life that test our faith and helps us to grow closer to the Lord. I have learned and really believe that God knows my every situation and every need. He is very forgiving and waits for me. If you think you have a hard time waiting on Him, think how long He must wait on us before we surrender to Him. Knowing that I don't have to be perfect. if I slip up, he forgives and forgets and moves on. He never loves us any less when we've slipped up because His mercies are new every morning. Great is His faithfulness to His children. He will also never leave us or give up on us.

FAITH – Many people struggle with having faith when things around them seem to go awry. What would you advise someone who wants to strengthen their faith?

My advice for someone who wants to strengthen their faith when things are going crazy, when you feel like there is no end in sight is to stop, look at the situation, breath, hold on and lean in tight to Jesus. You must remember that God has you, and you will get through this. God has a plan for you and He will help you through all difficulties in your life. I know it can be hard, trust me I have been there more than a time or two. It's like what my mom told me when I was having my firstborn and well into the 22 hours of hard labor I went through, she said "breath and just remember that with every contraction you are just one step closer to holding my new little life God is gifting me with. Think of something good and positive in your life, blessings that God has given you and thank Him for them. Don't let fear and doubt take over, because He said He would never leave us nor forsake us. Remember Phil. 4:8 "Fix your thoughts on what is true, and honorable, and right, and pure, and lovely, and admirable. Think about things that are excellent and worthy of praise." (NLT) He knows just how much you can handle, and it is then He takes over, so you can rejoice in His glory.

OVERCOME - How do you structure your time to reflect all the priorities and opportunities God has given you to be a light for him without losing yourself in the process, both personally and professionally?

Time management is not one of my strong points, so I must rely on God to see me through each day and to help me see the open doors and work he needs me to do. I have been raising kids for 32 years and I always knew what needed to be done. As someone would come along, God opened a door to witness or share something about my life that will encourage them, I take it. I don't go around trying to shove God down anyone's throat, but if the opportunity arises where I can share about Jesus, it just comes out. Same as it is now, as I go about my daily routine in home and working with my clients or at different events, I try to reflect God in everything I do, my attitude, service to others, smile on my face and caring for others. I love helping people. I try to remember that He put me in this place for a reason, to share His love and grace, to be kind and patient (especially with my clients). If I see a need I try to help just because I know it is the right thing to do and it makes not only that person feel better, but I feel better as well. If He gives me an opportunity (like this book) to share about Him and to help someone else with their walk with Him, I take it because it's not about me…. it's ALL about Him.

OVERCOME - Share with us about a season in your life that God sent you through that changed the course of your life.

It was when my oldest son was arrested on robbery and assault with a deadly weapon's charge and he was facing 30 years in prison. He had had an ongoing battle with drugs and blaming everyone for his choices. It was during this time of his incarceration in county jail and then going to trial, that I really had to let go and let God handle it. I was so exhausted from the past, that I needed to let God deal with his future. I went to Him with my heavy burdens and He let me rest in Him. He took away the worry and fear. I still had three other children at home that needed me, and He gave me a peace that was not of this world. I almost felt guilty at times because I wasn't all whacked out. After this time, God has placed in my heart to help other women that deal with this kind of pain. To share that if you let go and let Him take control, you can be at peace. Now I know that when things are really going south, all I must do is look up. The Lord has been so faithful to me, in keeping me by His side. He has been my rock and because of all this pain and trials, one after the other, I am better for it. Not only that, but God has used this to get my son's attention and he is eating up God's word, trusting Him to see him through this season of his life, knowing that he is being prepared for great things to come. Sometimes we don't understand the reasoning behind what God is allowing to happen in our lives, but it is just a season in which to grow, hold on, have faith and believe that the God of all creation, will see you through.

POUR -What three scriptures would you share with someone if they are in a season of transition and need clarity? Also, share why you selected these three scriptures.

Matt. 6:33 (NLT). "Seek the Kingdom of God above all else, and life righteously, and He will give you everything you need." This is one of my favorites because if you personalize it and own it, you can't go wrong. He will give you EVERYTHING you need. That means clarity and direction and all things needed for life personally and professionally.

Phil. 3: 13-14 (NLT) 13) …" I have not achieved it, but I focus on this one thing: Forgetting the past and look forward to what lies ahead, 14) I press on to reach the end of the race and receive the heavenly prize for which God, through Christ Jesus, is calling us."
I love this verse because it reminds me that I am not done. That I have to keep striving for the ultimate goal and stop looking in my past or letting life get in the way. I've got a crown of glory waiting for me.

Hebrews 10:23 (NLT) "Let us hold tightly, without wavering, to the hope we affirm, for God can be trusted to keep His promise."

That's exactly right, we can trust God to keep His promises. There is no doubt in my mind, because He is forever faithful.

Our hope and trust are in God. If you place all faith, hope and trust in the one who loved us first, who sent His one and only son to die on the cross for our sins, so we may have eternal life. Then there is no doubt He will see you through every obstacle and your victories will be without bounds. Hold tight to Him, He will see you through.

POUR -What is your favorite scripture, and how has that influenced your role as a woman who works and walks by faith?

I have so many it is hard to pick just one, but there is one that I base my faith and trust on and that is Rev. 1:8 (NLT). "I am the Alpha and the Omega-the beginning and the end," says the Lord God. "I am the one who is, who always was, and who is still to come – the Almighty One."

God is constant. Always and forever. He was before me and after me which means He is always there with us. My rock, my hope, my faith. I put my trust in the One who loved me first.

Any closing thoughts?

My faith comes from Christ alone. I am a very imperfect woman with a blemished past, but because of God's great of love for me, whose mercies are new every morning and whose grace is enough, I can live a redeemed life in Him. It doesn't matter where you've been, what you've done in your life…. God loves you so much and if you're having trouble whether it be personally or professionally…bring it to the cross. Lean into Jesus and follow the lead of the Holy Spirit, after all Jesus did send Him down to be our guide and counsel. And lastly, Trust in the Lord with ALL your heart and lean not on your own understanding!

I know who I am because: I am a woman of God, redeemed by Jesus Christ. I am loved, pursued and chosen, equipped with words of life. I am clothed in strength and dignity, commissioned here and now. I am gifted by the Spirit, FORGIVEN AND UNBOUND! Blessed is she who believes and Praise Jesus…. I BELIEVE!

VALLETTE HARRIS

Tell us a little about yourself.

I am a woman of the Christian faith. I regard my life to be committed to the Holy Trinity- Father, Son, and Holy Spirit. I was baptized at the early age of seven. I grew up in the environment where your elders would frequently question as to when you were going to get baptized. However, it wasn't until the age of twenty-eight where I encountered Christ on a personal level. It was that unforgettable encounter where I knew this was my experience and acceptance of Christ, and His salvation. I *needed* to give my life to Him. God had revealed Himself to me at a time where I was on a self-destructive path, which would have to lead me to prison, asylum or the cemetery. This was my truth. Since that moment in time, since my having experienced the saving grace and delivering the power of Jesus Christ, my life has not been the same. I have learned that I can enjoy life and be the woman God created me to be without compromising my faith. I enjoy all my favorite things to do and considering that I am entering the "prime of my life," I am looking forward to new adventures, and experiencing the next chapters of my life with the love of my life, my family, and friends.

Share with us what your business/ministry is and what it does for those that you serve.

I worked and served in ministry on a full-time level for approximately eight years. It was during this duration of time where I served as an intercessor and received ministerial licensure and certification to minister God's Word. I have been given what I consider to be a multi-facet ministry, where I serve in various areas such as intercession, biblical teaching/preaching and ministry administration. A vital aspect of my ministry consists of outreach about substance abuse/drug addiction, which gives me the opportunity to share God's word and my testimony with others who have experienced the same or related addictions.

DIRECTION - Sometimes people are confused in recognizing and knowing what they are called to do by the Lord. What advice would you share in how one can hear and know what God has called them to do?

Certainly, there are many avenues one can take to know what specific area of ministry and calling God as given to them. Be assured that as your relationship with God develops, it is through prayer and personal time with God where one can hear the leading and direction of God. He may direct you to specific scriptures, or you may be directed to seek godly counsel from your pastor or spiritual leader. I have found that there are several Christian websites that specifically address spiritual gifts and the five-fold ministries, even offering free questionnaires/tests that can assist you in learning and understanding who you are in Christ, and what area you find your self-drawn to in ministry. The Word of God is the best tool one can use to gain clarity. I Corinthians 12:1-11 address the Spiritual Gifts and Ephesians 4:11 address the Five-Fold Ministries

DIRECTION – There are times when someone may struggle with really knowing their gifts and how to use them. How did you know what you were gifted in, and how do you apply that in your life?

Initially, I learned of the Spiritual Gifts and Five-Fold Ministries during a biblical series regarding The Holy Spirit. My former Pastor dedicated our weekly bible study teaching on the Holy Spirit. I began to read additional books and materials concerning the gifts and callings, and as I began to volunteer in certain areas of ministry where I felt comfortable, I realized that God had revealed specific gifts within me. Ultimately, I came to know what I am gifted in which was a combination of teaching, prayer and receiving godly counsel from spiritual leadership who have the same gifts. The application varies from day to day, predicated on the mind of God, and when He chooses to use a certain gift through me. The basis of it all is supernaturally influenced.

DIRECTION - Many people struggle with developing a habit of including God in all that they do. How do you make God a part of your life/business/ministry each day?

I try to establish a disciplined prayer schedule that includes (early) morning, afternoon and bedtime. I listen to and "feed" my spirit with various worship songs and the Word of God throughout the day. There are some evenings before my bedtime where I read my favorite devotional or write my evening prayer in my journal. Finally, I am blessed to have a "core" of friends with whom I can pray with daily, discuss God's word, and what He is doing in our lives.

FAITH - As a woman of faith, what has been your biggest obstacle or challenge in your faith walk with God, and how did you navigate that successfully?

My biggest obstacle or challenge-**Letting go and getting out of God's way!**

I have deemed myself and my core circle of friends as "Make It Happen Women"! When you're a "make it happen woman", you stop at nothing to make things work out, fall into place, always finding options to solve issues and problems that come up whether in the home, ministry or your career. A "make it happen woman" spends a considerable amount of time planning, thinking, analyzing and researching to get the job done, meet the goal and setting things straight.

Then there are times when a "make it happen woman" encounters issues where she jumps into action, spinning at light speed changing from housecoat and slippers to military fatigues, rescuing, troubleshooting, quickly resolving. Well, that works for a time, but being a Woman of **FAITH**- you cannot lean on your own understanding, your own way of handling issues especially in a season of transition. As difficult as it can be, and as uncomfortable it can feel, a "make it happen woman" must learn to release her hand from the steering wheel and let Jesus take it! Growing into and walking daily as a woman of FAITH requires constant releasing and relinquishing some degree of independence to excel to a higher level of trust, confidence, and hope in GOD.

Every day, I live in the process of growing and maturing spiritually, placing my trust, hope, and confidence in God. To successfully navigate through life as a woman of faith, I am determined to stand IN and ON God's Word- HIS promises. I remind myself with the affirmations of who God has created me to be, and who I am in relationship to Him. I am constantly learning from life's hardships, tribulation, and self-inflicted wounds, that if I don't place my hope, trust, confidence and reliance in GOD, I am already dead because anything I attempt to do without Him has failed before it begins.

FAITH – Many people struggle with having faith when things around them seem to go awry. What would you advise someone who wants to strengthen their faith?

I will admit that when certain circumstances arise, when you're headed in a specific direction (life), and you believe that the way you're going is God ordained, yet somehow, things take a turn, it is difficult, initially, to not be shaken. I'll admit when things go awry, and plans are interrupted due to whatever the issue or circumstance may be, initially, your faith is affected. When I find that I am being challenged in my faith, I draw strength from prayer. I am strengthened by praying with understanding (English), but my faith is most definitely strengthened when I pray in the Spirit (heavenly language or tongues).

One can strengthen his/her faith by reaffirming the promises of God by speaking the promises of God out loud, making a declaration in prayer that God is for you and not against you. God is faithful. Recall how faithful God is and has been in the past, and in the present. Remind yourself of how faithful God is in ALL things, and not just some things. He is faithful, therefore, no matter what occurs and no matter how far off course we get, God promised that He should perfect, mature, bring to fulfillment everything that concerns us. His word declares that He strengthens us. The word of God holds the strength needed when things are thrown off course. It is vitally important to surround oneself with people of like mind, of like faith and greater faith. Be sure that you have a "core" "inner circle" of those who are on the same page with you and genuinely, authentically have your best interest at heart. You can draw strength from the "core", support system, which by the way should not incorporate many folks! Connecting with your "core", strengthens faith in times of testing and transition.

OVERCOME - How do you structure your time to reflect all the priorities and opportunities God has given you to be a light for him without losing yourself in the process, both personally and professionally?

The structure changes predicated on where I am in life and what my priorities are at that time. I structure my time to remain connected to my church family and my "core" or inner circle so that I am accessible and available to assist in ministry, even if I am available for a small duration of time, or only on specific days. I find that God will present opportunities to be a light for Him when I least expect it. Not losing myself in the process comes with growth, experience in ministry, learning how important balance is, and understanding that God desires a balanced life for us. There is a difference between "church work" and *the work of the church*. It is vitally important to know that there is a time for everything, and you alone cannot be everything for others, nor can you be everywhere all the time. I determine what I can handle effectively, and I establish boundaries. It is my experience that some of the most effective moments of ministry and being a light for God have been outside of the sanctuary (physical building).

OVERCOME - Share with us about a season in your life that God sent you through that changed the course of your life.

Several years ago, God spoke to me, and what he spoke to me was one word. I asked God if this was truly His voice speaking to me. I wanted to know beyond a shadow of a doubt that what I heard was God and not me! I even walked in different rooms in my apartment and stood still just to see if I was hearing God or the television! Nevertheless, it was God's voice, and from that moment I began to pray and converse with God on how this was going to work out for me. God relocated me. He orchestrated my exodus from one state to another, and it was truly by faith. It meant my having to start my life over in a place that I had never seen nor had even visited. God knew that for me to receive the blessings of both good times and hard times, being with and without, leaving the security of family and full-time ministry for the unknown would require my becoming totally dependent on Him.

Seasons of transition are not always comfortable nor compliant with your own plans and preconceived "blueprint" of how life will or should work out. Even when you have a vision or spiritual blueprint of how you will navigate in ministry, there will be seasons of transition where God will interrupt the "vision." God's turning you does not take you away from accomplishing that vision, but He determines how the vision will come to pass, or manifest. Seasons of transitions are not always comfortable, because this specific duration or period of life will require one to "painfully" learn how to release, and let go of what has become comfortable, familiar...letting go of the control device within your soul.

POUR -What three scriptures would you share with someone if they are in a season of transition and need clarity? Also, share why you selected these three scriptures.

Romans 8:28 *(Amplified translation)*, "We are assured an know that GOD being a partner in their labor, all things work together and are fitting into a plan for good to and for those who love God and are called according to HIS design and purpose."

When we come into seasons of transition, we must realize that this is God's way to cultivate character. He allows failure and disappointment to bring us to deeper degrees of humility because without Him; we can do absolutely NO THING. God reveals specific areas of our lives to us that is flawed, in need of pruning, purging and cleansing so that we become more Christ-like in our perspectives and behavior. We are always learning from our errors, becoming more aware of His sovereignty and unconditional love, His endless mercy, and grace. Seasons of transition helps us to grow in grace and increase in our personal, intimate relationship with Jesus Christ. We are benefactors of degrees of His wisdom and aspects of HIM that could not be revealed to us in one lump sum.

This is the trying or "stretching" of our faith. GOD is in no way short on memory, nor is He void of understanding who we are and where we are in life, however, we must know that His purpose and plan for us requires genuine, authentic trust and confidence in Him. We learn how to trust in God's ability to bring us into that predestinated place in life and His Kingdom. Transition, and all that comes with it does not always look as if God is working for our good. Most of the time, transition often appears as if God has forsaken us, left us out, overlooked or neglected us…some may even think that God does not love us, or we must have committed some heinous sin where there is no redemptive antidote. Beloved, not so. The seasons of luscious green and fruitful pastures, and the periods of barren, dry wilderness work together for our good. Determine to

a posture of faith and confidence that GOD has a
.ves, and HE will not fail us. GOD is not against us.

.roverbs 3:5-6 *(Amplified translation),* "Lean on, trust in and
be confident in the LORD with all your heart and mind, and do not
rely on your own insight or understanding. In all your ways know,
recognize and acknowledge HIM and HE will direct and make
straight and plain your paths."

In transition, it is imperative that we remain in a posture of
prayer, keeping the line of communication open and unfiltered
between our spirit and the Holy Spirit. It is vitally important that we
seek the face of God always, but even more in seasons of transition,
especially when we are not sure of what direction to take or know
what decision should be made regarding a specific issue. When I
find myself in a season of transition, I have come to learn that setting
aside time for prayer, fasting and reading God's Word helps to clear
my mind from the tumultuous thoughts and chaos of "the unknown".
I call these moments my "therapy sessions" because I approach the
Father, who is the Mighty Counselor, Psychologist, Psychiatrist,
whatever fits, and I lay it all out before Him!

Acknowledging the Lord is inclusive of choosing to confide in
Him, talking to Him about the what, where, who, when and how and
oh yes, the *"how long?"* I believe that as a woman Faith, it is
imperative that He gives me clarity of thought, asking God to speak
directly to my heart and spirit. God will give me direction and
sustain me wholly so that I can make it through and arrive
victoriously into the next dimension of my life.

There were times when I needed God to speak to me and direct me on whether I should relocate to another city, state or remain where I resided. There were certain aspects of my life that were changing, some for good and some were uncomfortable, but nevertheless, I knew that this was another season of transition for me, and I had to make sure that I would make the right move, the right decisions, and seek God for a plan of action.

Philippians 4:6 *(Amplified translation)*, "Do not fret or have any anxiety about anything, but in every circumstance and in everything by prayer and petition (definite requests) with thanksgiving, continue to make your wants known to God, and God's peace (shall be yours, that tranquil state of a soul assured of its salvation through Christ, and so fearing nothing from God and being content with its earthly lot of whatever sort that is that place which transcends all understanding shall garrison and guard over your heart and minds in Christ Jesus."

This has been one of my most treasured and beloved scriptures because the Apostle Paul, by the direction and divine knowledge of the Holy Spirit, addresses the vital need for us to seek the peace of God. He advises us to rail against negative thoughts and the cohorts of fear that we struggle with during transition. The state of our minds must remain in a place where faith can "guard" and watch over our tendency to become distracted by the "physical" circumstance, and how it appears to the natural or human eye, rather than how it appears to the spiritual eye.

'mes when seasons of transition can be very

ε, where you find yourself coming face to face with

...ances and situations that can very well make you feel and

...eve that you're going to lose your mind. Depression is an ongoing battle for some of us and in the "perfecting" process with our walk of faith we are learning how to rail against depression. We are victorious and growing stronger with each day. God is gently advising us, admonishing us not to allow doubt, anxiety, panic, depression, worry, and discouragement to overwhelm us. We must maintain our trust and confidence in Him, relying on what is the truth, seek His peace. The peace of God is without a doubt, far different from the "peace" we have defined as such. Walking by faith even during transitional times calls for action. We must continually pray, and not only give God our requests (asking) but without taking a pause, THANK HIM for hearing and answering, in every "thing" in every circumstance whether good or bad, up or down, illness or perfect health, debt or financially secure, single or married, pastor of 20 or 2,000...no matter what keep asking and thanking.

When you possess the peace of God, it will emanate from you so much so that those around you, who are aware of what you're going through, will think that something is wrong with you. You have the peace of God because you're not flipping out, wailing and holding your head in your hands as one being hopeless. The peace of God provides a degree of contentment that transcends, passes over depression, worry and panic because regardless of the perceived outcome, with God, **ALL** things are possible!

POUR -What is your favorite scripture, and how has that influenced your role as a woman who works and walks by faith?

There are several scriptures that I regard as favorites and most endearing for me, but if I have to select one, it would be Ephesians 3:20 (Amplified translation), "Now to Him who (by in consequence of) the (action of His) power that is at work within us, is able to (carry out His purpose and) do superabundantly far over and above all that we (dare) ask or think (infinitely beyond our highest prayers, desires, thoughts, hopes or dreams)."

There are moments of reflection where I find myself coupling this scripture with my thoughts and whispers to God. What I love about God's Word is that it is indeed the Bread of Life, and this scripture, when I begin to pull it apart, gently taking it in piece by piece, I am encouraged in my walk of faith. I am determined not only to desire big but dream big and expect big because whatever I can imagine, this word undeniably gives me a promise that only God can keep. As a woman who is walking and working by faith, not perfectly, but the influence through this scripture comes from God's unconditional love, grace, and mercy. I declare this word not only in my life but in the lives of those around me, the beloved that God has graced my life with. I not only believe that God shall exceed my expectations but the desires and expectations of all His people. This is the fuel that keeps the soul and spirit burning with the passion of Jesus Christ.

Any closing thoughts?

Part of my "spiritual makeup" is exposing the enemy! Allow me to do just that…. the diabolical strategy of the enemy is specifically designed to subtly chip away at your pillar of faith until you are left with a void, a hole in your soul and spirit. The enemy seizes every waking moment to "talk you into" walking *away* from God rather than walking *with* God.

We have become so comfortable and resilient in our human abilities and the way we process and disseminate information. We find ourselves navigating through life's seasons of rain, heat, cold and winds defaulting to what we have been programmed to do. Having faith in ourselves and others is easier than having faith in God. Why? Because God is not governed by human abilities and time, and we would rather "microwave" our way through life rather than experience the value of waiting, developing patience and longsuffering. The major component to becoming a woman of FAITH is the object of her affection, the one who has captured her heart~ The Father, The Son and The Holy Spirit- one Sovereign Creator who will never die. God has no beginning and has no end He is all-knowing, all-powerful, infinitely and miraculously ever present. We were destined for greatness! Believe in God and believe in yourself as a child of God! God is not asking us to be perfect but to persevere. Let go and Let God!

VICTORIA
SOTO

I have been blessed to be in a position to be asked of my faith and to profess to whom I belong. This must be synonymous with who I am and how I should identify myself to the world and my identity as a whole. It is in the reflection of Christ is where we should ponder our attempts of beauty where it truly counts and exist. If we can but look to Jesus Christ, our Lord and savior as our example, as ordered and commanded in love, that we will find the peace, courage, will and joy to face the day to Day challenges we all face on this plane of existence we call earth, our temporary home.

When I was asked to be a co-author and contribute to this series, I couldn't say no. If you understand, and I know you do, what it is like to be stretched from pillar to post with work, family, social/civic duties and yes, our service missions in and out of the church, you would say, there is simply no time. I say all this before I give you a proper introduction of myself, so you can get to know a little about me beforehand because it simply felt natural for me to start this way.

I am Victoria Soto, JD. I am also, Mrs. Victoria Soto, wife, Vicky, daughter and sister, Victoria, friend and what I believe to be a most precious handle, Mom, mother of a son, who will be eleven in less than a month from my writing these words. I am also a mother of amazing grown men and women, which means I am also known as Victoria, Nana to beautiful grandbabies. I am called sister in life and sister in Christ, along with friend and counselor. To some, near and dear to my heart, I am called Miss Vicky/Victoria, no relation to the brand name or product of popularity. By trade or career, I have been blessed to have been a licensed attorney for more than 20 years and a published author regarding my professional law practice and career. Along with being a published author for faith-based books that I pray will inspire and encourage other women of faith to find the peace in the struggle, affirmation in their walk and to focus on their great value in the individual uniqueness and purpose or purposes that God created them for. Who am I to write these words and hit the notes that I mentioned above?

Well, I am simply a child of God who has a will to serve him and he in his infinite love has provided this as a "way". I am just like any woman who has faced challenging times, unspeakable pain of loss and desolation through my life and because time and time again my God sees me through. I know there is a light that only he can bring that lies on the other side of the mountain of pain and strife that any of my sisters see themselves in from one day to the next. I have discovered that one of my missions and/or purpose in life is to share with others the value I see in them that they may not have seen in themselves. Additionally, I strive to be a beacon in a dark place that they may find themselves traveling through. My work as an attorney gives me the honor and privilege to help others through times of strife and hardship. We all see hard-times and live it. We have been ordered to gather together, support one another in this life for a very specific reason and that our God has a plan for us. We were all created for such a time as this. Each sister going through struggle can learn from one another and lean on one another. We lean on one another so that we find ourselves being held upright in times that we would undoubtedly fall flat on the floor of life. I tell you, it is by our Lord God's design that we were created to be survivors as a testament to God's glory and to one another. This tells us that if one of us can do it, then we all can.

The questions that our amazing compiler has laid out for us to address in this book will help me to focus on what words I may impact on the reader and will hopefully inspire, enlighten and awaken what it is that God wants us to wake up and see.

To the questions I pray to be courageous and bold in my answers and that in these answers that I too am so blessed by what God will reveal to me as I take part in this God inspired project.

DIRECTION - Sometimes people are confused in recognizing and knowing what they are called to do by the Lord. What advice would you share in how one can hear and know what God has called them to do?

I love this direction and the question that comes with it: We all know who the author of confusion is. It is in the forgetting of what and who brings about confusion that we find ourselves falling into the traps of confusion, especially when it comes to recognizing and knowing what our Lord God has called us to do in this life. Remembering that confusion in anything is not what our Father wants for us and remembering that it is the exact mission of what the enemy desires for us is the first step in repelling away confusion and finding your focus. I have found through experience and having been blessed by strong leaders of faith that the best step to take in repelling any confusion is to first focus on God and the knowledge that he is a living God who is not only a Heavenly Father but a warm and attentive Father. He created us for a unique reason, fashioned us with a love that we can merely begin to imagine and is with us and sees us as we are in all our moments. When we focus on him through our confusion in purpose and life, that focus shatters the confusion, silences the noise of the naysayers, and hustle and bustle that is meant to distract us from our purpose. Once that noise and confusion is quieted and disappears sisters then ask yourself, what special gifts has God blessed me with and how can I use them to bless others? Did you see that word "others"? Did you think that the answer to your purpose was going to be about you? Wow, I did! I thought this was about me, that my purpose was about me. What was I meant to achieve, to be, to get, that God had planned for me? No! How powerful is that? How simple the answer is and yet so revealing and rewarding when it is revealed that to find your purpose and mission is to discover how your special gifts were given to you to serve others and in the serving, you become the human being, the soul, the supernova "you" that he, our Lord God created you to be. Stepping out of your comfort zone and taking that leap into the greatness you were created for in a way that when you let go and recognize what has come easy to you all along was put in you in that way so that you could be part of something greater than self. the purpose of love and freedom that God has planned for us all. So, with me, I knew that as I grew to experience one thing after another one of my constant gifts was that of being a natural encourager. I was able to see a beauty in my fellow sister or brother and to share with them that vision. I have always had a need to ease another's pain through words of truth delivered in a way where they could receive it with an ease of comfort and not as a criticism or a blow, depending on the message. He gave me the gifts of "words".

DIRECTION – There are times when someone may struggle with really knowing their gifts and how to use them. How did you know what you were gifted in, and how do you apply that in your life?

Sometimes, we "struggle" with recognizing our gifts because what we thought of as a curse or a bad habit has been a gift from God in disguise. Therefore, do a little self-reflecting exercise and ask yourself what, in your mind are your pluses and minuses, your pros and cons. Then do a little cross reference. Step back and ask yourself, how can the minuses be used to glorify God? It is easy to see how the pros can glorify him. However, when you use this formula on the negative traits you thought you possessed you may be surprised that these were the hidden gems of your gifts that once uncovered and viewed through the eyes of a loving God who would only bless you and not curse you, Wow! You have unlocked your purpose. For example, well, there is no delicate way of saying this, I have the gift of gab, seriously, I talk at warp speed. I have known this. How I have survived all these years by being able to count on one hand how many times people have told me to shut up, it can only be God. I have screamed inside my head at least once a day for the last 50 years, "girl, you need to shut up, you know you are getting on these people's nerves", but I keep talking. God has blessed me with this gift of gab that has served me, my work and my mission to pray like I am saying my last words and if I don't get it all out I may not finish what God put me in this moment to finish. So, for years what I thought may have been a curse I slowly realized when I focused on God that he created me this way to serve others. You may or may not have heard people refer to attorneys as "mouthpieces", well now you know, you must speak for others who may not have the ability and sometimes do not have a voice to speak for themselves. So, ask yourself or remind yourself of those abilities that you may have always possessed and or have cultivated extremely well like a duck to water. In that discovery or realization, you may find that you are walking in your purpose and or can now ease into it because God has given you the gift that is the key to unlock the purpose you were created for.

DIRECTION - Many people struggle with developing a habit of including God in all that they do. How do you make God a part of your life/business/ministry each day?

I gave the example above regarding my way through the fog of discovering my gifts. And how by focusing on him I found my way through the confusion to now using them for purposes that God created me for. In my daily life and work, focusing on God and making that a habit by calling on him in all things from the moment that I step out of my house and into my car to drive, I am constantly praying for his mercy and grace. I pray for the protection of my family, my ability to care for those he puts in my charge, who I may be working with, representing, speaking in front of professionally or who I may run into at the grocers. Prayer is the tool and gift that I use to stay connected to him through it all. I apply it when the going gets rough and the seas become rocky. I call on him with a wailing sound of need and confidence. Even though there is peace and confidence in knowing that he is with me, we live in what can be a cruel and cold world. Where we are sometimes in seasons of illness and strife and we are waiting and dreading for the proverbial other shoe to drop. When it does it can be and has been and I expect in the future that it will again be devastatingly crushing. So, my habit to keep myself focused on him is a daily and dedicated prayer.

FAITH - As a woman of faith, what has been your biggest obstacle or challenge in your faith walk with God, and how did you navigate that successfully.

I had to first get over the obstacle of forgetting that I was not in the struggle alone. When I found myself alone and broken from life, I had to remember who loved me first. I had to remember that this life was so great that he laid down it all so that distraction and defeat would not be how my story would end. I had to remember all that he had ever done for me through the times of my life when I thought that I might not live to see another day. I had to remember that the person that I loved more than anyone on this earth would likely not live to ever see again and would be leaving me alone in this world with no one to love me unconditionally as only a mother could as my mother loved me. I had to remember the truth and that was that I was not alone, far from it. We tend to forget that he walks with us. More importantly, that he walked for us in the 33 years he walked and lived among us. He came here not only to die on the cross for our sins but to do so fully he had to be born of flesh like us. He experienced hunger and hurt like us, felt disparity and loneliness like us, and understood hunger and thirst like us. We forget that he wanted to understand what our pain felt like, what it would feel like when we would go through it because he walked in our shoes many years ago so that he could know and relate to us. He wanted to be with us and for us and survive it with us and hold us and walk us through it today. Hear me sisters. When we focus on who our God is to us, it breaks that cycle of self-pity we all tend to go through at times. Once we break through that gigantic obstacle of forgetting the enormity, the lovely real Lord God we serve, we can move on with a sigh of relief that he knows and that we are not alone.

FAITH – Many people struggle with having faith when things around them seem to go awry. What would you advise someone who wants to strengthen their faith?

As a child and an adult, I felt isolated, odd and alone because of my situation of poverty and at times of abuse. Being belittled by life's circumstances and the trial of lies that were told of my not being worthy of what God has called me to be because of someone's opinion of what my place in this world should be, I had to remember my true origin of being a daughter of the everlasting all powerful God. We are sisters and women of royal descent. This is how I strengthened my faith and found my center, through remembering who I am in Jesus Christ and who he is in me. (Philippians 4:13 Scripture, I can do all things through Christ, who strengthens me) When I identified where I came from and who created me, this is how I survived. This is how you too will survive the strife and hard times that this world will throw at us.

I remembered that my Lord Jesus was with me then. Before I was a twinkle in this universe he knew me and loved me enough to get to know me. He did this by choosing to come to this earth, to live as a human being and then making the ultimate sacrifice. I remembered that as a daughter of the King, I am naturally a princess and royalty thus walking this earth. In that knowledge, I was able to hold my head up high and say no more to the abuse, no more to the lies and strife and forever no more to the loneliness because of what lies in me, the Holy Spirit left in me as a gift by our Lord God after he made the ultimate sacrifice and gave his life for us that we may have everlasting life lived abundantly. Remembering that He that lives in me is greater than he that lives in this world is my way and it is also yours. Grab it sister and use it to navigate through the troubled waters. We will walk through knowing who is wading in these waters beside us.

OVERCOME - How do you structure your time to reflect all the priorities and opportunities God has given you to be a light for him without losing yourself in the process, both personally and professionally?

I find this question a little perplexing, which makes it very interesting to me. Being structured by having a strong prayer life and having been blessed by God and having a tower of prayer warriors around me through my life. Prayer is the lifeblood of a strong spirit filled life. This life is one of great love for God and if your love is true and giving it proves itself and shows itself in a successful life, well lived. When your life is one that it is well lived, your light for him is not only illuminating from your life as an example to others but this light is one that nourishes you so that you are not diminished in its brilliance, but you live free in his love as he would have you. The part about the question that perplexed me, if that is the right word is the part about not losing yourself. It is my belief that you are never more than yourself than when you are living as light for him. there is such love and peace in the knowledge that you are doing the right thing and overcoming what comes your way. It is not easy, and the burden is not always light, but the joy in achieving that blessing of light when you live for him is when you will know who you are and not be lost but instead, be found.

OVERCOME - Share with us about a season in your life that God sent you through that changed the course of your life.

I reference this above which was the time my mother went to be with Jesus. It was a season that we all face in one way or another, the loss of a loved one. It was unexpected because she was my super hero mom. She had survived countless similar surgeries, so what reason did I have to believe that she would not survive this one? She died to this earth to be present with God and serve him in heaven and what made that moment pivotal and life changing to me was the fact that God showed me the strength that he had put in me to survive it. I came through this time because of who God was in me. Instead of turning into myself and closing down, I used the gifts that God gave me to survive and serve others to take the focus off me and lay it at the feet of God. Another realization that I went through was any given situation that I find myself in is not mine to control, it is God and his work is solid and his faith is unmatched. Therefore, this realization was freeing.

POUR -What three scriptures would you share with someone if they are in a season of transition and need clarity?

I would share the following scriptures with anyone out their struggling:

"I can do all things through him who strengthens me!" (Philippians 4:13) Put on the full Armor of God... "gird yourself." (Ephesians 6:11) Another verse would be John 3:16, "For God so loved the world that he gave his only Son so that we may have life and more abundantly...," I selected these scriptures because they have been repeated as part of my daily prayer and declaration of faith to my Lord God and as a woman who respects power, these scriptures are very powerful. When I focus on the power that is harnessed in these scriptures there is such clarity in the truth that none of my success and gifts that he has bestowed on me is about me but what God would have me to do for him with them. This deep understanding gives me purpose and peace and direction and the knowledge that there is the promise of love lived well because of God's love abiding with me and mine. These scriptures speak power into whatever you need to feel and accomplish, and I apply them in my work day to Day.

My most favorite would be put on the full armor in my work as it is many times a prepare for battle cry when I put on my attorney's suit to protect and defend. However, in my day to day life, I would have to lean to "I can do all things through Christ who strengthens me!

For the peace and grace of the world and all those whom I love it is the John 3:16, ... For God so loved the world that he gave his only begotten son. There you have it. It was hard to pick so I categorized my three favorites and when they come into play. They have all in one way or another influence my walk-in life and in my work.

Any closing thoughts?

Remember that there is a God victory in whatever you may be going through. When our Lord Jesus gave his life on Calvary, the victory for all there was to be defeated was won and all the victories of the challenges yet to come are won! We are walking from the battles. The victory is won!!!

Love you, Amen!

KATHY FOGARTY

Sometimes, people are confused in recognizing and knowing what they are called to do by the Lord. What advice would you offer in how people can hear and know what God has called them to do?

Get rid of the clutter! I'm typically very organized, and I try to be the same way in my spiritual walk. In doing so, I've learned to declutter! Recognizing your calling means having clarity of vision; this requires purging through the "clutter" in life that muddles spiritual vision. Although some "clutter" can be us saying "yes" to good things, we need to be careful it doesn't become an obstacle blocking the path to our calling. So, seek God about what has you so busy and distracted that you can't hear Him or see His leading.

Also, movement gives way to clarity. When Jesus said, "Be still and know that I am God." He was referring to *knowing* who He is and will be for you. He wasn't saying, "Do nothing and I will show up." How do we move forward? By getting to know God through seeking Him in prayer, in His word and in His service. Being a Sunday school teacher to toddlers might lead to your calling as a Ladies' Ministry Leader. Providing food and helping with cleanup for church fellowships could lead to your calling in a street ministry helping the homeless. When you feel God speaking to you to attend a certain event or help in an area you don't feel equipped to do, **go**!

It has taken some purging, decluttering, praying, seeking, listening to God, and moving forward over the years to help me come to the point of living on purpose for His purpose.

Purging, seeking and moving will lead you to knowing.

There are times when someone may struggle with really knowing their gifts and how to use them. How did you know what you were gifted in, and how do you apply that in your life?

Since I was a child I enjoyed writing poetry which led to songwriting. Then blogging led to becoming an author. As I grew in the Lord, I recognized my passion is my gift. Seek the Lord and ask yourself, "What do I enjoy doing? What puts a lump in my throat when I am serving in that capacity?" That might be your gift. Using my gift of writing opened the door to other gifts; as a singer, speaker, and ministry leader. The gift of exhortation is involved in each one. The gifts don't all happen at once; they can come in seasons. Staying "in tune" with God helps me to be open and ready when God says, "It's time."

You're not alone; I struggled, too. Although I loved writing, it was hard to write a poem in school for a classmate or a paper in creative writing. It was hard to find the right words to fit a melody. It was hard to write a blog I had no idea how to do. It was hard to sit down at the computer and write a book without experience. It was all hard *in my head* until I started. It was hard until I let go of what I could not do and began to believe what God could do through me. Looking back, God was preparing me for the "now." He's always in the "now" and has the best at work for your future. *Embrace what lies before you in confidence of what God can do through you.*

Many people struggle with developing a habit of including God in all that they do. How do you make God a part of your life/business/ministry each day?

What I have learned is it's all in choice. Then, choice turns to habit. It's important to be careful of what we tell ourselves, such as,

"I'm not good enough," "I don't have experience" or "I'm scared, so I won't do that today." Our thoughts are very controlling of our calling; whether we act on God's calling or rest in our thoughts.

Also, respond instead of reacting with what your schedule *becomes.* I am a "list" person and sometimes that list will change without notice! We all have good intentions on our "To Do" list, but our list might get "God interruptions" for His calling in the moments, daily doings.

So, we need to let the choices we make be based on the beauty of God's grace and who we are in Him and remember His plan is perfect. How? **Begin each day with the armor of God.** The Helmet of Salvation will help you take every thought captive for Christ. *"And take the helmet of salvation..." Ephesians 6:17* **Be open and ready to follow God's lead**. *Yahweh is better than your way. "Many are the plans in the mind of a man, but it is the purpose of the LORD that will stand." Proverbs 19:21 (ESV)*

As a woman of faith, what has been your biggest obstacle or challenge in your faith walk with God, and how did you navigate that successfully?

Struggling with "self" has been my biggest obstacle. Breaking that down reveals pride and trust issues. It is amazing how we have the knowledge of who we are in Christ, but do we really *know* it and exercise that gift? Plus, I have asked myself, "What am I saying about who God is?" That spoke to me and shed light on a calling Satan wanted to shut down. So, what has worked for me in pushing through that obstacle is committing to giving *at least* 30 minutes a day applying myself in working toward that goal of complete surrender to Christ and His calling for me. By listening intentionally to the direction of the Holy Spirit and sitting down at the keyboard to write everyday has given me such freedom; complete surrender. When I am there, the walk is sweet.

Many people struggle with having faith when things around them seem to go awry. What would you advise someone who wants to strengthen their faith?

Resist, Revisit, Restore, Renew

Resist-Again, the Armor of God is so important to apply each day. The "Shield of Faith" protects from the flaming arrows (things that go awry) catching you off guard and weakening your strength.

A few years back, I was disappointed in a choice someone very dear to me made that affected me in a depressing way. I was losing sleep and unhappy. Then one morning in my quiet time the Lord spoke to my heart and said, "Don't live in other people's choices because it is taking away the joy I'm trying to give you today." Wow! That changed my outlook then and still does today! So, we also must resist living in other's choices. Wake up *hungry* for God's plan and ready to receive His joy!

Revisit-Dwell in God's word seeking and asking Him to reveal the promises He wants you to *feast upon* daily.

Restore-Print those promises God reminded you of during your revisit on 3x5 card or paper, put in your daily reading or on your bathroom mirror. Read them every day and put your name within the text. Let God speak to you through His word. *Savor* His scripture.

Renew-Each day is a day to renew. By daily resisting, revisiting and restoring, a renewing of your faith will begin. Then suddenly, *you will notice no matter what is served that day, you are **satisfied** in Him alone.* Your faith has strengthened.

How do you structure your time to reflect all the priorities and opportunities God has given you to be a light for him without losing yourself in the process, both personally and professionally?

Having an accountability partner is important because of all the chaos we can get swept up into and before long Satan has used darkness to taint or destroy your testimony/calling. Whether it is personally or professionally, my husband is my accountability partner and I am his. This is a learning process no matter if it is your spouse or a friend. With the approach of love through it all, we've not only learned each other's weaknesses but also discovered each other's strengths. God puts people together to bring out the best in them. Connect with someone that does that for you.

Also, following the **Fruit of the Spirit** has been a good guide. I have intentionally displayed it in my living room to read and apply daily. It is also a good reminder during the day when situations seem to be challenging. "But the fruit of the Spirit is love, joy, peace, longsuffering, kindness, goodness, faithfulness, gentleness, self-control. Against such there is no law." Galatians 5:22-23 (NKJV)

Having accountability and God's reminder of how we should walk this life helps in staying grounded and focused for our good and His glory.

Share with us about a season in your life that God sent you through that changed the course of your life.

We lived in Texas where my husband, David, was pastor of a small church. He also had a full-time sales job and without warning the company shut down. He was hired by other companies and either the department he worked for dissolved or the company would shut its doors. It was evident God was moving, so we let go of our will and walked in His daily presence. Although it was hard, because of total submission to His will there was such a sweet peace; the eye of the storm.

In the meantime, a large local church approached us about merging. We prayed, talked, and followed God's direction and merged.

Due to the financial strain, we put our house on the market in May of that year. Since the market was bad, we figured it would take at least six months to sell.

My son, who lived in Arkansas, mentioned there was a job fair David might be interested in checking out. We went. David got a job. In two weeks, our house sold, and we moved to Arkansas at the end of June.

Our granddaughter, Briley Faith, was born that October, and never took a breath on her own. She had a muscular disease she fought for 61 days. God's plan was to get us to Arkansas, so we could be with her every day up until she went to her heavenly home.

From that, God molded me into a calling as an author beginning with a story of faith.

What three scriptures would you share with someone if they are in a season of transition and need clarity? Also, share why you selected these three scriptures.

Trust *His way.*

"Trust in the LORD with all thine heart; and lean not unto thine own understanding. In all thy ways acknowledge Him, and He shall direct thy paths." Proverbs 3:5-6 (NKJV)

On my desk is a picture of Briley's hand in mine. Resting on that picture is a "scripture rock" that has Proverbs 3:5-6 engraved upon it as a gentle reminder. We didn't know "why" she passed away at 61 days, but we knew "Who" we could trust. During this transition, I learned to lean on the One who knows best. Through that journey of total trust, I received clarity to my calling and "Who" became greater than "why."

Visualize *His best.*

"And the LORD answered me: "Write the vision; make it plain on tablets, so he may run who reads it. For still the vision awaits its appointed time; it hastens to the end—it will not lie. If it seems slow, wait for it; it will surely come; it will not delay." Habakkuk 2:2-3 (ESV)

God's timing is perfect, so, it's worth waiting on His best! This scripture is displayed at my desk to remind me to wait on God's best. During times when it seems my desires are depressed, and nothing is happening, I've learned to remember God is always at work and His "best" is coming!

Wait *expectantly.*

"In the morning, LORD, you hear my voice; in the morning I lay my requests before you and wait expectantly." Psalm 5:3 (NIV)

I rejoice in knowing God hears me and I can *expect* Him to show up!

What is your favorite scripture, and how has that influenced your role as a woman who works and walks by faith?

Ephesians 6:14-18 "Stand therefore, having **girded your waist with truth**, having put on the **breastplate of righteousness**, and having **shod your feet with the preparation of the gospel of peace**; above all, taking the **shield of faith** with which, you will be able to quench all the fiery darts of the wicked one. And take the **helmet of salvation**, and the **sword of the Spirit**, which is the word of God; **praying always** with all prayer and supplication in the Spirit, being **watchful** to this end with all **perseverance and supplication** for all the saints."

There are several scriptures I would deem as my favorite. But the Lord put it on my heart to share this favorite.

The armor of God, found in Ephesians 6:14-18, is a very important resource God gives us to withstand evils and struggles while building a stronger faith foundation. I believe God did not put the scripture there as an *accessory as desired,* but as a *necessity required* for each day. This application has strengthened my faith in God, and my confidence in who I am in Him: an inside-out transformation; a soldier of faith prepared for victory.

Any closing thoughts?

Just remember the smallest step might turn into the biggest step in your life. *Trust is a must.* Decide to walk even when you cannot see.

"For we walk by faith, not by sight." 2 Corinthians 5:7 (KJV)

ALLISON UNGER

Tell us a little about yourself.

My name is Allison Unger and I currently reside in Dallas, TX. I grew up in a town called Friendswood, which is a suburb south of Houston. I received a Mass Communication degree from Texas State University and have been in Dallas since 2012.

I currently work as a production manager in the corporate video production world and love everything about it. Every day is different, every day is a challenge, and every day I get to do what I love.

I'm an introvert by nature, but my job and ministry call me to be the opposite quite frequently. Friday nights you will find me at home alone getting lost in a new TV show or movie. Apart from work, I am an amateur screenwriter and write any chance I get. I hope to one day be able to write and produce content with a purpose.

I absolutely love to bake, and I always say that if my writing career fails, my backup plan will be to open a bakery.

I became a Christian at a young age, but it's been full of seasons of ups and downs, of refinement and refreshment and taken me on a journey I never could have predicted.

Share with us what your business/ministry is and what it does for those that you serve.

I serve with a ministry called Reclaimed, which exists to empower and mobilize God's church to redefine a hyper-sexualized culture, restore men and women victimized by the sex industry, and to reach a world hurt by the abuse of sex all through the power of

Jesus Christ. The sad reality is that sexual exploitation happens in every city in the U.S. and around the world, but an even sadder reality is that most people are unaware of it.

Reclaimed serves victims of sexual exploitation through many avenues. I specifically serve with our motel outreach team. Since trafficking and prostitution happens frequently out of motels, we go to different motels in the Dallas area and engage with motel staff to educate them on the signs of trafficking and show them what they can do to help report the activity.

Within every story of trafficking or prostitution, is a string of devastating circumstances that caused each woman to be there. The ultimate answer is the loving power of Christ and we see that power on the frontlines every day.

DIRECTION - Sometimes people are confused in recognizing and knowing what they are called to do by the Lord. What advice would you share in how one can hear and know what God has called them to do?

This is such a great question and an issue that is still a struggle for me. For years, I begged God to tell me what He wanted me to do. I prayed for clarity, I prayed for specifics, I prayed for God to make it easy.

I felt a calling to write, specifically for the screen, but I refused to move forward with writing until God laid out exactly what I was supposed to write and how it would be used. It took me years of frustration to realize that I was asking the wrong questions.

I was already writing, albeit poorly and with the wrong perspective, but instead of screaming for clarity, I should have humbly asked for guidance and moved forward on faith. I was too distraught in my own self-pity and crippled by fear that I wasn't listening to God.

It's hard to move forward with a project, script, or whatever it is that you do, without knowing what the result will be or how God will use it. But I guess that's where the concept of faith comes in.

If you're struggling with what God is calling you to do, I'd start by looking at what you're passionate about and what you like doing. For me, God took my passion, turned it into a calling and molded it to fit His purposes.

Ephesians 2:10 says, "For we are His workmanship, created in Christ Jesus for good works, which God prepared beforehand that we should walk in them." God uniquely created us and therefore uniquely gifted us. Look at what God has given you a passion for and pray for God to use it.

However, don't confuse "passionate about" with being "successful at." Those are wildly different things. If I based my writing on how "successful" I was, I would have stopped writing soon after I started, because from the world's perspective, I was a failure. I'd also caution to not expect that passion to come easy or without any challenges.

Successful means something different to the world than it does to God. You're calling is not to satisfy you, it's to glorify God and once you start working from that perspective, frustration and fear no longer hinder your progress.

If you still feel that you're not hearing from God, I'd say seek the Lord. Before you roll your eyes that I just gave you the classic Christian cop-out answer, hear me out. The Bible calls us to abide daily and seek the Lord always. When you are in communion with God daily, either through prayer, in the Word, or with fellow believers, He is going to speak to you in ways that you would miss if all your prayers are prayers of frustration that God isn't speaking to you. God speaks to us constantly; we just have to be in the right mindset to hear Him.

When God is your first call and not your last resort, you're going to see God in more of your life because you are inviting Him into more of your life.

DIRECTION – There are times when someone may struggle with really knowing their gifts and how to use them. How did you know what you were gifted in, and how do you apply that in your life?

From a young age, I have always been a huge movie and TV fan. I think I loved the escapism factor that a story can bring, being able to transport me to another world and make me feel something. In high school, that love of story manifested in a lot of acting, but in college, my focus turned more behind the camera and slowly to writing. Towards the end of my college years, I attempted to write my first screenplay - attempted being the key word.

I never particularly liked writing before, but felt it was something I needed to do. If I'm being completely honest, I hated it at first. I absolutely hated it. Everything about it was frustrating and my story went nowhere fast.

After I graduated college, I didn't really write for about a year and half. I was busy starting my career and since writing didn't come easy, I didn't see the benefit of it, so it took a backseat. But after looking to my professional career for purpose, I came up empty and the desire to write came back up.

I still wanted to work on the story I started in college. I knew that if I really wanted to make a go of it, I had to be all in and dedicate my time to writing. When I finally surrendered my time to God and began to write daily and truly focus on my craft, God completely changed my perspective on writing.

Even if you're gifted in something or feel called to do something, that doesn't mean it necessarily comes easy or that it won't bring its fair share of burdens. Writing, specifically screenwriting, takes practice and daily discipline. In the beginning, I wasn't willing to put in the time because I wanted it to be quick and easy and, it was long and exhausting.

I heard a phrase in a sermon once - "Embrace the lonely discipline." That concept stuck with me and I think it's applicable to everyone, regardless of calling. Using your gifts, whatever they may be, will take time. Time spent alone working on your craft, time that no one else sees. Learning to "embrace the lonely discipline" changed my perspective.

Now I cherish the quiet nights when I'm in my writing room, getting lost in a story. Yes, it's still frustrating and exhausting at times, but now I love writing. Not because I'm great at it, but because I know God has called me to it and fulfilling that calling is satisfying beyond words.

I know we all want God to clearly lay out what our gifts are and tell us exactly how to use them for a certain ministry, but that's not what we signed up for when we surrendered our lives to Christ.

God works seemingly slow at times, but incredibly fast at others. You must learn to be still in the times of waiting and ready to jump into action when God calls.

DIRECTION - Many people struggle with developing a habit of including God in all that they do. How do you make God a part of your life/business/ministry each day?

Once you have an idea of the direction God wants you to take, it's easy to make decisions and keep moving forward without asking for continual guidance. It's easy to forget that God is your source of strength.

Personally, I need the constant reminder that God is in control because it is second nature for me to get my marching orders and run full steam ahead without checking in with God along the way. I get an idea and run with it. Then I wonder why I find myself completely spent as I've exhausted my strength before I've even begun to tap into God's strength.

If I don't start my day in the Word, I'm setting myself up to take on the wrong perspective for the day. Once I walk out the door in the morning, my email will start going off, people will need me to do something and if I don't start my morning with the right fuel, I'm less likely to turn back to that source of truth throughout the day.

If you find yourself completely exhausted, frustrated and you feel like you're not making any progress, ask yourself if you've prayed through the problem at hand or are you panicking prematurely. Just like writing is a daily discipline that I had to learn, so is staying in constant communication with God.

A go-to method for me is to do a prayer walk around the block. Something about walking helps focus my prayers and the exercise is always much needed. It's amazing what a good prayer walk or just a moment of stillness in the Lord can do. It can shift perspectives, diminish fears and refresh you to continue in the fight.

FAITH - As a woman of faith, what has been your biggest obstacle or challenge in your faith walk with God, and how did you navigate that successfully?

For as long as I can remember, I have struggled with Obsessive Compulsive Disorder. The biggest obstacle of my faith was being able to say that out loud. I was so ashamed of the stigma behind it that I kept it a secret from everyone around me. The thing about secrets is they keep you from moving forward because you are so focused on keeping your secret that you don't notice the things and people around you.

I finally came to a place where I just couldn't do it anymore. I was exhausted from keeping this secret and feeling like I was living two different lives. I came to a place of surrender and realized that if I didn't deal with this, I couldn't move forward with God's plans for my life.

This moment lead me to Regeneration, a biblically based, twelve-step program through Watermark Community Church. It was the first place I felt safe sharing knowing that I wouldn't be judged. God took me through a challenging year, as I learned to own the hurts that my secret had caused those around me and how to surrender to God daily and trust that He is fully in control, regardless of circumstances.

Since taking the step to come out of hiding with my OCD, my life has never been the same. There's such a sense of freedom in not carrying around that secret baggage anymore.

If I never would have dealt with my OCD, I'm not sure I would have had the motivation to turn back to writing, and if I didn't turn back to writing, I'm not sure my path would have led me to combat sex trafficking.

FAITH – Many people struggle with having faith when things around them seem to go awry. What would you advise someone who wants to strengthen their faith?

Practice, patience and perseverance.

Faith is a discipline and I think that discipline is learned in moments where nothing is going right, and a positive outcome seems impossible.

It's in those down moments when you really have to dig in and trust that God has you in His arms. If we trust God in the good times, then we have to trust Him in the bad. God is in control 100% of time, even in the times it seems like He's not.

When you became a Christian, God transformed you. But being a daily follower of Christ, God continues to refine you, which seems to be more painful. And for me, this comes through faith. Once I became a Christian, I had the misconception that I needed God less, but, the opposite is true. God cleaned up the major things when you trusted your life to Him, but then comes the smaller, more subtle sins, which are harder to admit and harder to let go of.

Hard times are hard times in the moment, but one day you will look back and realize that you needed that hard time to get you to this point of success or clarity today. Pain has a purpose; it's just all about perspective.

OVERCOME - How do you structure your time to reflect all the priorities and opportunities God has given you to be a light for him without losing yourself in the process, both personally and professionally?

Learn to say no. Easy right? It's incredibly difficult for me to turn down any kind of opportunity to be a part of something or lead a ministry. I am often stretched thin over too many things and I'm not being effective at any of those things. That doesn't serve others well and it certainly doesn't serve me well.

Just because an opportunity arises, doesn't mean it's what God wants for you. This is a lesson I still have not fully mastered. There are things you may like doing, but you have to ask yourself if they are taking you away from what God has called you to do. Discernment comes into play and if you're not abiding daily, clarity on priorities can get muddy quite quickly.

When I find myself begging God for more time in the day or complaining that nothing is coming easily, I must step back and weigh my list of tasks against God's. When I do, I realize God has given me all the time I need, I'm just doing things with my time He hasn't called me to do.

When I think I have it all figured out, I tend to move full speed ahead without bringing God along with me. If I don't start the day in the Word and end my day in prayer, I'm setting myself up to be overworked, under productive and physically spent. Make a list of priorities, pray through them, and God will make very clear what should be on it, and what should be crossed off the list.

OVERCOME - Share with us about a season in your life that God sent you through that changed the course of your life.

So, remember that screenplay I started back in college? Well, through much frustration, many revisions and countless hours later, I completed it. And you know what became of it? Nothing. Nada. Not a thing. This was a true breaking point in my walk with God. I was at an utter loss for direction. I felt God had taken me on this incredibly long and painful journey and I came up completely empty.

I questioned if writing was even my calling at all and felt like I had spent years chasing after nothing. I didn't understand how I could have spent so long on something and have God not come through. But in my darkest hour, I heard that still small voice. I realized that God still wanted to use my story, just not in the way I wanted it. I had to let go of my plans, so God could execute His.

Through many circumstances that are beyond the context of this book, God planted the idea of turning my script into a short film. It was painful to let go of the hours upon hours spent dreaming of what this script would look like produced. The thought of taking my 112 pages that I had painfully scoured over and turning them into 10 measly pages made no sense. But like I mentioned before, God works at incredibly slow paces at times and incredibly fast paces at others. From the time this thought was planted through final production was five short months. In that time, I rewrote the script to fit the short format, fundraised, casted, hired my crew and produced my first short film. If I would have known back in college that this script I was working on was only going to be made into a short film, I would have stopped right there. At that moment in time, it would have made no sense, and only looking back on the entirety of the journey can I see the clarity to God's seemingly nonsensical plan.

I had to take the back roads for God to get me going in the right direction and I think that's true for a lot of us. We can only see what's right in front of us, but God sees our future. So instead of fighting Him the whole way, roll down the windows and enjoy the ride, whatever road He takes you on.

POUR -What three scriptures would you share with someone if they are in a season of transition and need clarity? Also, share why you selected these three scriptures.

1 Corinthians 15:58 - it's easy to let criticism, setbacks and disappointment keep you from continuing the work God has called you to do. You may work months, years or decades without seeing the full fruits of your labor, but this verse is a reminder to keep a heavenly perspective and gives an assurance that your work in the service of the Lord is not without purpose.

James 1:2-4 - patience, a fruit of the spirit I'm sure a lot of us felt we had more to give. Serving the Lord will automatically test your character, faith and patience. This verse shifts the perspective of seeing problems as setbacks, to seeing them as growing opportunities. God promises to see us through trials, all we have to do is be willing to show a little patience and trust in His sovereignty.

Esther 4:14 - when my life seems to be in utter chaos where nothing seems to be going my way and I don't see a way out of my present circumstance, or if I'm in a season of waiting and I feel like I'm not hearing from God, this verse is a great reminder that God is in control and I am not. While I can only see what's right in front of me, God sees my past as well as my future and is orchestrating my life to serve Him. You never know when God has you where you are for *such a time as this*.

POUR -What is your favorite scripture, and how has that influenced your role as a woman who works and walks by faith?

I'm going to have to piggyback off 1 Corinthians 15:58. I first became aware of that verse when I volunteered one summer at a Christian camp in high school. It was on the back of our volunteer shirt. I didn't realize the significance of that verse at the time. However, the influence of that verse in my life is undeniable and that shirt still sits in my dresser.

Choosing a career in ministry, whether full or part time, will bring its fair share of criticism and challenges. Some of that criticism will come from outside the church community, but some that hits closer to home. Some unfounded, some well-intentioned, but all hard to keep you from second-guessing your choices.

I love the bold statement at the top of this verse - "Stand firm." So simple, but so powerful. There's been many occasions when it felt like no one was on my side and I had to stand firm in my convictions, but stand firm alone, which can be a scary place to be. But in those standing firm moments, are some of the sweetest I've had with the Lord, as I've experienced His power at work in my life like never before. These moments always seem to precede a major working of the Lord.

Serving the Lord always comes with its fair share of sacrifices. Giving yourself "fully to the work of the Lord" sometimes means someone that you care about gets less than the full you. That can be hard to bear at times but knowing that your work in the Lord "is not in vain" brings everything back into perspective.

This verse is my daily source of fuel. It's pinned to my wall and not a day goes by that I don't meditate on that verse. It reminds me to stand firm in my convictions, dig in for the long haul, and take comfort knowing that God is walking right alongside me.

Any closing thoughts?

Looking back from where I am today, I never could have predicted the circuitous journey God has taken me on. Only now can I appreciate how all the pieces worked together to get me to where God needed me to be. In the moments of confusion and chaos, I couldn't appreciate God's beauty in it and failed to recognize its purpose.

Somehow, in God's all-knowing, all-powerful way, He took me through the trial of OCD, which somehow reinforced my passion to write, which led me to fight for victims of sex trafficking and prostitution. The crazy thing is that He's not done with His plan for my life. Who knows what the next season, the next chapter, the next calling God will place on my heart and the roundabout path He will take me on to get there.

I know it can seem daunting to discover God's will for your life but remember that nothing you do or don't do will hinder God's plans. He will accomplish through you what He set out do, it's up to you if you're going to fight Him every step of the way or surrender fully to Him.

Whether you're still searching for your initial calling or feel like you've hit a dead end with where God has you right now, all I can say is pray hard, pray through and be ready for God to take you on a journey you never could have imagined, doing something you never could have predicted.

95686924R00137

Made in the USA
Middletown, DE
29 October 2018